Additional Praise for

Knowledge Management: A Guide for Your Journey to Best-Practice Processes

"APQC's new Passport to Success series is a real hit. The format is loaded with information that is easy to understand as well as easy to use. It is full of actionable data. *Knowledge Management* is extremely helpful— I can't wait to see the next book in this series."

JERRY GASS
DIRECTOR, QUALITY PROGRAMS
USAA

"This book is an excellent reference guide for the complex world of knowledge management and will be of great value to both new and seasoned practitioners. It furnishes the reader with real-world knowledge management examples, roadblocks to success, and recommended approaches that can be readily leveraged within any organization. I particularly liked the use of checklists at the end of each of the landmark chapters."

PHIL PERKINS, PH.D.
SENIOR DIRECTOR, KNOWLEDGE MANAGEMENT
THE PILLSBURY COMPANY

"Many books give me the theory on how to do something, but when I try to implement it, I don't understand where to start—much less which questions I should be asking myself. Not only does the *Knowledge Management* Passport book tell me how to do it, the "Check Your Status" section asks all the thought-provoking questions that I must answer to be successful. Finally ... a tool that really is handy!"

PAT BEHRENS
MANAGER, BENCHMARKING
NORTEL NETWORKS

"APQC's *Knowledge Management: A Guide for Your Journey to Best-Practice Processes* is unique in that it explains the topic of knowledge management in such a straightforward way. Unlike many writings on this topic, it explains knowledge management so that everyone can understand it. At the same time, it serves as a helpful guide to those who are already working toward implementing better knowledge management practices."

WENDY FINNERTY
CORPORATE QUALITY MANAGER
BASF CORPORATION

"APQC has built an outstanding reputation for making complex subject areas meaningful, understandable, and actionable. APQC's Passport to Success book on knowledge management continues this rich tradition. *Knowledge Management: A Guide for Your Journey to Best-Practice Processes* provides valuable and relevant information on various facets of knowledge management based on practical experiences of industry practitioners. Most importantly, it provides you with guidelines to develop your own road map for successful implementation of a knowledge management program within your organization. This publication is helping us leverage the collective intellect of practitioners in this field."

BIPIN JUNNARKAR
VICE PRESIDENT, KNOWLEDGE MANAGEMENT,
AND CHIEF KNOWLEDGE OFFICER
GATEWAY INC.

APQC'S PASSPORT TO SUCCESS SERIES

Knowledge Management

A GUIDE FOR YOUR JOURNEY TO BEST-PRACTICE PROCESSES

Carla O'Dell, Ph.D.

Susan Elliott

Cindy Hubert

AMERICAN PRODUCTIVITY
& QUALITY CENTER

American Productivity & Quality Center
123 North Post Oak Lane, Third Floor
Houston, TX 77024

Edited by Susan Elliott
Designed by Connie Choate

Manufactured in the United States of America

ISBN 1-928593-22-4

American Productivity & Quality Center
Web site address: http://www.apqc.org/

Contents

Acknowledgments

The American Productivity & Quality Center (APQC) would like to thank all of the organizations we have worked with to uncover the trends and best practices in the growing world of knowledge management. Without the companies that sponsor our research—and especially those that are willing to impart their knowledge, experiences, and insights—we would not be able to share this valuable information with the public.

We would also like to thank the APQC employees who have spent long hours and put in much hard work to make our research and studies successful.

Finally, a special thank you goes to the contributors of the Traveler's Tips—those practitioners who were willing to share their expertise in this book—and to Amy Price at Schlumberger for acting as a sounding board for our ideas.

Preface

E ver since the American Productivity & Quality Center formed in 1977 as the American Productivity Center, our goal has been to disseminate knowledge to help organizations perform more effectively. We've done that in numerous ways over the years, from developing improvement and measurement approaches to offering benchmarking studies, conferences, training courses, research services, and a variety of publications.

Recently, our members and other customers have told us there is an emerging need for easy-to-use resource guides to help them communicate, understand, and implement programs and processes in a variety of functional areas. As a result, we've drawn on our experience and knowledge to produce APQC's Passport to Success book series.

We chose the title Passport to Success because these books are intended to guide you on what can be a difficult journey through somewhat foreign territory. Each book in this series provides readers with the mechanisms to gauge their current status, understand the components (or landmarks) of a successful initiative in a specific topic area, and determine how to proceed within their own organization.

These books also supplement the other "hands-on" support services and products APQC offers, so that we may provide you with integrated process improvement tools. To learn what else APQC provides in your area of interest, please visit our Web site at www.apqc.org or call 800-776-9676 (713-681-4020 outside the United States).

Introduction

APQC defines organizational knowledge as "valuable information in action," with value being determined through the eyes of the organization and the recipient. If people don't have a context for the information or understand how to use it, the information is not valuable and therefore cannot be considered knowledge. Today's organizations have a wealth of information and data embedded in them, but that information doesn't become knowledge unless a human being or group of people can add context to it and put it into use.

Most scholars agree that knowledge comes in two forms: *tacit*—which includes experience, know-how, skills, and intuition and is most often embedded in the individual—and *explicit*—which is information you can easily put into words or pictures or that is easy to articulate and communicate. Both are essential to an organization and must be captured and shared for others to benefit.

Knowledge management, then, becomes the conscious strategy of putting both tacit and explicit knowledge into action by creating context, infrastructure, and learning cycles that enable people to find and use the collective knowledge of the enterprise. As we discovered in our first study on knowledge management in 1996—and have

reinforced through subsequent studies and research—the process
usually involves several of the following stages or subprocesses in the
use of knowledge: create, identify, collect, organize, share, adapt, and
use (Figure 1).

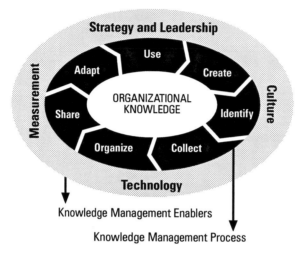

Developed by APQC and Arthur Andersen in 1995

Figure 1

WHY MANAGE KNOWLEDGE?

The simplest way to explain why most organizations want to
manage their knowledge is that it is a means to achieving their
mission, whatever that may be. Among those factors influencing the
increasing proliferation of knowledge management are market forces
such as:
- the need for speed and cycle-time reduction;
- revenue growth;
- competition for customer relationships;
- lost knowledge from turnover, hiring, downsizing, and restructuring;

- the fact that knowledge has a higher margin than product; and
- globalization.

Other reasons for managing knowledge have to do with infrastructure capabilities, including:
- the rise of powerful network, communication, database, and collaborative technologies;
- the understanding of tacit and explicit knowledge; and
- change management and process skills.

By exploring the "why" factor with the organizations we've studied, we've arrived at six major strategies for knowledge management:

Knowledge Management as a Business Strategy: This strategy is evident in organizations that feel strongly that knowledge management and sharing are key to their ability to compete and grow. These organizations often see knowledge as their product and pursue knowledge management because they firmly believe it will have a significant, positive impact on the profitability of the enterprise. Consulting firms are one example.

Transfer of Knowledge and Best Practices: This is the most widespread strategy. It focuses on systematic approaches to the reuse of knowledge and the transfer of best practices, with the goal of using this knowledge to improve operations, products, or services. Sharing this tacit and explicit knowledge enables an organization to operate more effectively and efficiently.

Customer-Focused Knowledge: This strategy focuses on capturing knowledge about customers; developing and transferring knowledge and understanding of customers' needs, preferences, and businesses to increase sales; and using the knowledge of the organization to solve customers' problems. It recently has come to include enabling customers to access the organization's knowledge to find solutions to their problems on their own.

Personal Responsibility for Knowledge: Organizations operating under this strategy believe that people are the engine of knowledge and should be supported in, and responsible for, identifying, maintaining, and expanding their own knowledge. They also are expected to understand, increase, and share their knowledge assets. These organizations realize that their employees are their most valuable asset and need to be able to use their knowledge—both personal and that of the collective enterprise—to benefit the customer and the company. There also is a trend toward making teams and communities of practice responsible for critical bodies of organizational knowledge.

Intellectual Asset Management: This strategy emphasizes enterprise-level management of intellectual assets such as patents, technologies, operational and management practices, customer relations, organizational arrangements, and other structural knowledge assets. Effective exploitation of these valuable assets can help the organization increase its competitive advantage. There is an emerging movement to measure the value of organizational knowledge assets.

Innovation and Knowledge Creation: This strategy emphasizes innovation and the creation of new knowledge through basic and applied research and development. The development of unique knowledge and expertise increases the organization's competitive value.

No matter what your organization's reasons for managing knowledge, one statement rings true: *Ensuring that the right people have the right knowledge at the right time simply makes sense.*

Where Are You Now?

The following quiz is designed to help you determine the current state of knowledge management at your organization. Answer these questions, and then score your organization based on the scale on page 7 to find out where you're starting from.

1. Is your organization doing anything it calls knowledge management?

   Yes ☐ No ☐

2. Is there a general consensus in your organization about what knowledge management means?

   Yes ☐ No ☐

3. Is your organization doing something that, although not called knowledge management, falls under the definition of knowledge management (either the one your organization uses or the one presented in this book)?

   Yes ☐ No ☐

4. If knowledge management is occurring, whether at the grassroots or the organizational level, does it have senior management support?

   Yes ☐ No ☐

5. Does senior management understand and support knowledge management as a key to your organization's business strategy?

   Yes ☐ No ☐

6. Are people specifically assigned to knowledge management activities?

Yes ☐ No ☐

7. Does your organization as a whole know what knowledge it already has?

Yes ☐ No ☐

8. Do the people who need it know who has it and how to find it?

Yes ☐ No ☐

9. Is knowledge systematically transferred from one part of your organization to another?

Yes ☐ No ☐

10. Is knowledge consistently gathered from outside your organization for internal use?

Yes ☐ No ☐

11. Is technology used to effectively share knowledge within your organization?

Yes ☐ No ☐

12. Are people networks used to effectively share knowledge within your organization?

Yes ☐ No ☐

13. Does the culture of your organization encourage people to share their knowledge and reward them for doing so?

Yes ☐ No ☐

14. Is your organization taking full advantage of its knowledge to improve its products and services?

Yes ☐ No ☐

15. Does your organization measure the impact or success of its knowledge management efforts?

Yes ☐ No ☐

Number of "yes" responses _____

SCORE YOURSELF:

0–5 "yes" responses: Take out your compass and get ready to embark on an exciting journey. While you obviously have recognized the benefits of knowledge management, you've got a significant amount of work ahead of you to incorporate the necessary concepts and processes. The good news is that many people have forged this path ahead of you, and you can take advantage of the lessons they've learned along the way to ensure that you're heading in the right direction. Read on to learn more!

6–10 "yes" responses: You're on the right path to taking advantage of what knowledge management has to offer, but you have many areas yet to explore. Your next step is identifying the areas in which your organization is weakest and focusing your efforts there, and you can use the Landmark chapters that follow to help. Once you strengthen those areas, you'll be amazed to discover how much greater the impact of a well-rounded knowledge management strategy is.

11–15 "yes" responses: You're well on your way to demonstrating best practices in knowledge management. Your "no" answers will indicate the areas in which your organization needs to improve. Even if you answered "yes" to all 15 questions, as you read the following chapters, ask yourself what more you should be doing to strengthen each of the components. The goal is not just to be able to say you're addressing a specific facet but rather to say you're doing it well enough that its positive impact is felt throughout your organization. Remember, any practice—knowledge management included— must be diligently revisited and improved upon if it is to deliver its maximum benefit.

Knowledge Management Landmarks

We consider the following to be the landmarks, or key components, you'll encounter and need to address on your knowledge management journey. They are defined here in general terms and are explored in detail, as they relate to knowledge management, in the following chapters.

i.   *Value Proposition:* the business rationale, unique to your organization, for embarking on an initiative or instituting a process.
ii. *Culture:* the pervasive, yet usually unwritten and unspoken, rules and expectations that guide the actions of an entire organization.
iii. *Structure and Roles/Responsibilities:* the way an organization is set up, as that set-up relates to a process or an initiative, and the associated positions and tasks of its employees.
iv. *Information Technology:* the electronic tools that help an initiative or a process occur.
v.   *Approaches:* the tactic(s) you take when embarking on an initiative or beginning a process.
vi. *Measurement:* the process of gathering data and assigning value to the impact of a process or an initiative.

Value Proposition

Sharing knowledge and best practices because it's "the right thing to do" or because everyone else is doing it won't get you very far. To benefit from knowledge management, you have to have a goal in mind—that is, know *why* you're doing it. And that goal must link to the growth of your entity; otherwise, the initiative stands a good chance of being cut by upper management even if you view it as a success.

This is where the value proposition comes in. It provides a unique business rationale for embarking on a knowledge-enabled change journey, and it enables organizations to ensure that they devote valuable resources to high-payoff areas, that the "right" knowledge is managed and transferred, and that they get management's attention—and funding.

APQC has studied and worked with more than 100 organizations that have defined clear value propositions for their businesses. The focus areas have tended to fall into three general categories:
- customer intimacy,
- product-to-market excellence, and
- operational excellence.

Value Propositions

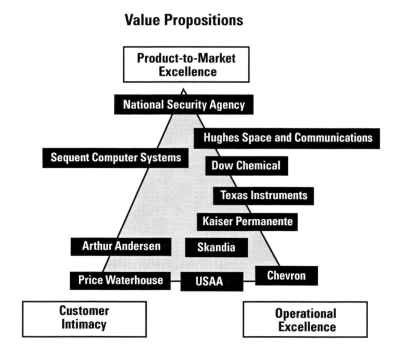

Based on a model developed by Treacy and Wiersma, *Harvard Business Review,* Jan./Feb. 1993

Figure 2

Figure 2 shows a graphic representation of the value propositions of the best-practice organizations examined in APQC's first benchmarking study on knowledge management.

CUSTOMER INTIMACY

Customer intimacy involves capturing and using companywide knowledge about how to market, sell, and service customers more efficiently and effectively. Many organizations that operate under this value proposition arm their front-line employees with the collective intelligence of the organization and use them to gather information from their customers as well.

For instance, USAA, an insurance and financial service organization, has implemented a comprehensive customer feedback system that quantifies customer feedback and improves overall knowledge of the customer. The knowledge and transfer system performs two primary functions:

1. It lets every service rep know all there is to know about a customer or a problem and provides the rep with the current "best practices" for addressing an issue; and

2. It tracks customer satisfaction on an ongoing basis, reveals regional and other trends, and shares performance measures with each employee so that everyone knows "how they're doing" all the time, every time.

PRODUCT-TO-MARKET EXCELLENCE

Speed has become a driver of business change. This means there is less time to procrastinate on new product ideas and to rerun experiments or try out new products before a full launch. *Product-to-market excellence* focuses on three transfer strategies: 1) ensuring new ideas and new designs from inside and outside the organization are

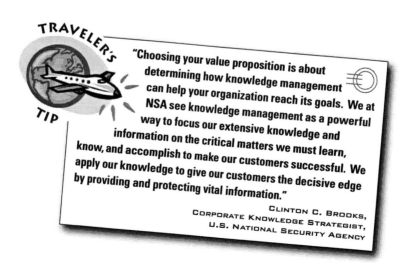

TRAVELER'S TIP

"Choosing your value proposition is about determining how knowledge management can help your organization reach its goals. We at NSA see knowledge management as a powerful way to focus our extensive knowledge and information on the critical matters we must learn, know, and accomplish to make our customers successful. We apply our knowledge to give our customers the decisive edge by providing and protecting vital information."

CLINTON C. BROOKS,
CORPORATE KNOWLEDGE STRATEGIST,
U.S. NATIONAL SECURITY AGENCY

incorporated into product and service offerings, 2) accelerating the product development process by reusing lessons learned from earlier attempts, and 3) collecting and disseminating competitive and market information internally, where speed is crucial. By reducing time to market, designing and commercializing new products more quickly and successfully, and staying abreast of the competition, organizations can increase revenue, retain market lead, and grow profit margins.

For pharmaceutical corporation Eli Lilly and Company, reducing time to market is a critical driver of success. Lilly's value proposition focuses on bringing new drugs to patients more quickly and cost effectively by improving global sharing of knowledge among Lilly employees. The company's Project Management Workbench contains project-specific information, cross-project perspectives, and tools and techniques that allow anyone on a drug development team, senior management, or line management to share product development information. Cycle time for distribution of this information has decreased substantially through this initiative, and this, in turn, helps decrease the time and costs associated with drug development.

OPERATIONAL EXCELLENCE

Companies following *operational excellence* as a value proposition want to boost revenue by reducing the cost of production and increasing productivity—raising performance to new highs. The transfer of operational processes and know-how from top-performing business units to those businesses performing less optimally is critical to achieving operational excellence.

As a result of developing a "repeatable" process to launch new businesses by sharing operational best practices across the company's global business units, Skandia insurance company has shrunk the lead time of starting a new business to seven months (vs. the prior industry standard of seven years). Skandia reuses existing expertise and "best tricks" from established business units to start up new ones. The organization has seen a reduction in cycle time and tremendous savings in new business start-up costs.

ROADBLOCKS TO SUCCESS

- Overlooking the connection to the revenue "value chain"—the key processes that make money for the organization
- Goals and focus of efforts are so decentralized that everyone uses his or her own
- No flexibility built into the focus strategy
- Focus is matched with the wrong knowledge management approach
- Senior leaders and/or key stakeholders are excluded from focus selection

It is important to note that many organizations have more than one value proposition that leads them to knowledge management and sharing best practices. The focus of healthcare product manufacturer Johnson & Johnson, for instance, includes elements of each of the preceding categories. According to Michael J. Burtha, director of knowledge networking, Johnson & Johnson uses knowledge networking to support the creation and delivery of new products and services to benefit its customers, as well as to support company growth and innovation.

DETERMINING YOUR OWN VALUE PROPOSITION

Determining which one of the three value propositions is best for your organization depends on 1) where the greatest potential for improvement may be, and 2) your firm's competitive strategy.

The easiest way to choose your focus area, or value proposition, is to look for the highest pain or the highest gain. The classic methodology for targeting improvement work and investment involves identifying the highest costs, the greatest revenue potential, and the biggest competitive threat. After you find those, you'll know where to focus your knowledge capture and transfer efforts for the biggest payoff.

But no matter what focus you ultimately pursue, keep in mind that markets, business environment, customer preferences, and even your own operations are dynamic. Adapting your focus when the time comes is as critical as choosing the first course of action.

 **CHECK YOUR STATUS**

1. What is your organization's business strategy?

2. What are your organization's core business processes?

3. Where are your organization's "high-gain" or "high-pain" functions and/or core processes?

4. Are improvement projects under way to address these functions and processes?

5. How could valuable knowledge or best practices enhance these processes if they were accessible or used in a different manner?

6. Is knowledge management already explicitly part of those processes?

7. Does your organization want to transfer knowledge and best practices around:
   • customers, their needs, and their expectations;
   • products/services, the speed of innovation, and speed to market; or
   • operational excellence, improving internal processes, and employee skills and competencies?

8. Who are the key stakeholders for the knowledge management initiatives?

Culture

Every organization has its own culture—the unique combination of expectations, written and unwritten rules, and social mores that dictates the everyday actions and behaviors of each employee. Culture is perhaps the most important factor in the success of your knowledge management initiative, and it is definitely the most complex to change.

Few organizations are lucky enough to start off with cultures in which sharing and collaborating come naturally. The more likely scenario is that people are motivated and rewarded to use their knowledge to excel personally. While this benefits the company to some extent, it doesn't come close to delivering the results that occur when knowledge is collected and used to advance the organization as a whole.

Numerous reasons related to culture account for the lack of knowledge sharing in organizations. Participants in our 1999 Creating a Knowledge-Sharing Culture study indicated that the biggest impediments are lack of time dedicated to transferring knowledge and an environment that fosters the "not invented here" (NIH) philosophy (Figure 3, page 18). In this chapter we explore the somewhat difficult, but not impossible, path to overcoming these obstacles.

Impediments to the Implementation of a Knowledge-Sharing Approach

People do not have the time to share knowledge. — 3.4

We have a strong not-invented-here culture. — 3.1

Our organization is divided into many divisions. — 2.9

People are scattered geographically and it is difficult to connect. — 2.7

People are afraid that sharing knowledge will make them less valuable to the organization. — 2.5

There is an unwillingness to share. — 2.5

Our organization is unaware of the importance of knowledge sharing. — 2.3

Leadership does not care about sharing knowledge. — 2.1

We have significant legal constraints. — 1.8

Scale: 1=small impediment, 4=major impediment

n=23

Figure 3

Throughout our research, we have seen that as companies move beyond the barriers and start sharing their knowledge—whether in a grassroots effort to transfer valuable information on a small scale, perhaps in a certain project, or through an organizationwide mandate handed down from top management—they begin to discover how profitable collaboration can be. Once communities of practice or cross-functional teams are engaged, the norm of sharing knowledge begins to self-perpetuate.

WORKING WITHIN YOUR CULTURE

Knowledge management initiatives have little chance of changing the overall culture of your organization—nor should they be used for such a purpose. They also don't stand much of a chance if they're positioned simply as a new activity or direction for the company. Best-practice organizations have demonstrated that knowledge management and sharing succeed most often when they link to a pre-existing core value. When collaboration and communication build on core values already embedded within the company, it means less of a change and, therefore, a more natural step for everyone involved.

For instance, the culture at software company Lotus Development Corporation is very informal, from the way its employees dress to the ad hoc teams that collaborate to work on a project or a product. In addition to this informality, Lotus has other cultural characteristics that naturally complement knowledge-sharing activities. Employees feel free to test their ideas and then modify them within Lotus' forgiving environment. The company perceives change as a positive and places significant value on the out-of-the-box thinking that can foster it. Finally, Lotus demonstrates a low tolerance for reinvention and rediscovery when a solution already exists somewhere in the organization. All these cultural aspects combine to create an environment that is ripe for knowledge management and transfer in Lotus. This will differ in other cultures.

So what do you do if your organization's culture isn't conducive to sharing? No matter if you're a senior manager or a member of the rank-and-file work force, your first step is the same: Lead by example. Every organization values success, so share your knowledge with others as a means of attaining that goal. While your actions will have more impact the higher up you are in the company, you have the power to influence the culture of at least the group you interact with most closely, be it a team, a department, or an entire enterprise. When people around you see how much they benefit from your knowledge, they'll naturally want to add theirs and see where the combination can take you—together. And remember, a grassroots initiative that demonstrates success is one of the best ways to get senior leadership on board and to buy in to your philosophy.

RESPONSIBILITY AT THE INDIVIDUAL LEVEL

The second step is to ensure that individuals have the tools, the time, and the incentive to contribute to and leverage shared knowledge. Again, this is most easily achieved by those at the highest levels of the organization, or at the head of a department or group, because they have the most overarching influence. Therefore, if you are starting a knowledge management initiative at the grassroots level, you need to find an upper-level champion who can provide these necessities. Likewise, if you are an upper-level champion, you need to secure buy-in from those who will be doing the work.

REWARDS AND RECOGNITION

In a perfect world, the benefits of accessing and contributing knowledge would be intrinsic. In some organizations, in fact, they are: People who share knowledge are better able to achieve their work objectives, can do their jobs more quickly and thoroughly, and receive recognition from their peers as key contributors and experts.

Other companies, however, need to create more structured rewards and recognition systems to encourage their employees to change their behavior where knowledge is concerned. Whether these rewards are tangible or intangible, they are a means of acknowledging the value of sharing knowledge, appreciating the contributions people make, and increasing awareness about the importance of not hoarding what you know.

American Management Systems (AMS), a business consulting firm, uses a combination of tangible and intangible rewards for participation in its knowledge system. Employees desire to be recognized as "associates," or internal subject matter experts, and therefore strive to make contributions that present a compelling case for their nomination and confirmation as an associate. AMS publicizes the contributions most in demand in an online newsletter and at associate gatherings. The company also hosts a Knowledge in Action contest, sponsored by IBM/Lotus, through which employees can receive cash awards for showing the value of the knowledge they've leveraged throughout the year.

No matter how your organization chooses to reward and recognize employees for their role in knowledge management, make

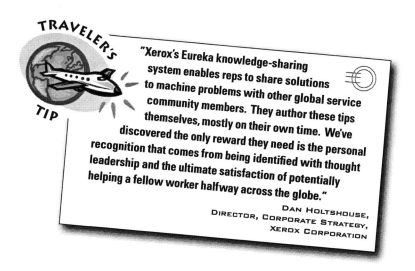

TRAVELER'S TIP

"Xerox's Eureka knowledge-sharing system enables reps to share solutions to machine problems with other global service community members. They author these tips themselves, mostly on their own time. We've discovered the only reward they need is the personal recognition that comes from being identified with thought leadership and the ultimate satisfaction of potentially helping a fellow worker halfway across the globe."

DAN HOLTSHOUSE,
DIRECTOR, CORPORATE STRATEGY,
XEROX CORPORATION

sure it aligns with and is supported by your culture. If knowledge sharing isn't inherently rewarding, celebrated, and supported by the organization, then "token" awards will be viewed as worthless and may actually have a negative effect.

INTEGRATING KNOWLEDGE MANAGEMENT INTO WORK

In 1997, when we conducted our Using Information Technology to Support Knowledge Management benchmarking study, only two of the surveyed organizations indicated that knowledge management was part of their actual work processes. In our most recent study, however, all of the best-practice organizations indicated that sharing ideas and getting help from others who have the necessary knowledge is an integral part of their work processes.

Where these latter best-practice organizations differ, however, is in how they integrate knowledge sharing into each worker's daily activities. Many make knowledge sharing—both accessing and contributing—a routine step in everyday work (Figure 4).

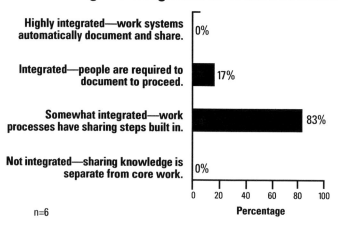

Degree to Which Capturing and Sharing Knowledge Is Integrated in Work Processes

Figure 4

At PricewaterhouseCoopers (PwC) consulting firm, for example, knowledge sharing is part of daily activities as employees rely heavily on each other's insights to do their jobs. The success of a project depends on the employee's ability to discover who within PwC has the information required by the client. PricewaterhouseCoopers' human networks and easily navigated information technology tools provide this type of information quickly and efficiently. Therefore, although PwC employees seem to find personal satisfaction in managing and sharing their knowledge, they do it largely because it is necessary for survival in the organization.

Several leading organizations also host knowledge-sharing events—highly visible gatherings during which people exchange knowledge, insights, and practices—to shape the behavior of their employees and make it clear that the organization values the transfer of knowledge.

ROADBLOCKS TO SUCCESS

- Lack of common perspectives
- Lack of time
- Non-aligned reward systems
- Lack of motivation (source)
- Lack of absorptive capacity (recipient)
- No formal communication; ad hoc only
- More emphasis placed on explicit knowledge
- Technology and the knowledge to use it are not adequate

CHECK YOUR STATUS

1. What percentage of people in your organization understand and appreciate the importance of sharing and transferring knowledge to your business strategy?

2. Is your organization team-based?

3. Do people in your organization see sharing knowledge as an important part of their jobs?

4. Are people in your organization given the time to interact—to share insights, experiences, and best practices?

5. Is the capture and transfer of knowledge integrated into your work processes?

6. Do people know how to use the common tools, systems, and technology?

7. Do your organization's work systems require people to document (e.g., trip reports, project evaluations, and lessons learned)?

8. How often do people use the documentation produced by your work processes?

9. What aspects of your organization's culture (values, beliefs) complement sharing knowledge?

10. What are the top three barriers to transferring knowledge in your organization?

Structure and Roles/Responsibilities

S uccessful organizations intuitively realize that they cannot manage or transfer their knowledge unless they have an explicit and institutionalized infrastructure in place. Without a structured process, and people with well-defined roles within that process, an organization's knowledge will not be used to its full potential.

Throughout our studies and projects, we have discovered that knowledge management in best-practice organizations is usually described as a management responsibility, supported by a shared infrastructure. This infrastructure may include:

- one or more knowledge champions who provide the coordination, develop the shared vision, and offer facilitation and encouragement;
- a common information technology platform;
- space—physical, cognitive, and social—to encourage sharing; and
- a corporate repository, such as a library or a database.

In this chapter we focus on the roles and the organizational structure, such as the organizational chart and reporting relationships, that facilitate the sharing and management of knowledge. Communities, or networks, of people are explored here, as well as in the Approaches chapter of this book. Information technology, a key enabler of the knowledge management infrastructure, is addressed in its own chapter.

ORGANIZATIONAL STRUCTURE

Many companies that excel at knowledge management assign the associated responsibilities throughout the organization as it makes sense and as required by their strategies and goals. Those that treat knowledge management as a business strategy, for example, tend to have extensive and widespread resources devoted to making knowledge sharing possible, and even easy, for all employees.

The organizational charts of these companies reflect their sweeping dedication to knowledge management. For instance, Fujitsu Network Communications, a designer and manufacturer of fiber-optic transmission and broadband switching platforms, has constructed its organizational chart so that knowledge management and work force development report to the senior vice president of quality, customer service, and information technology. As a result, the company views knowledge management holistically, rather than as a specific initiative set off by organizational boundaries and therefore limited in its success.

National Semiconductor Corporation, a developer and manufacturer of semiconductor products in the electronics equipment industry, started its knowledge management efforts at the grassroots level. Its Corporate Information Services group introduced and rolled out search engines and document management tools, and the Engineering group began using communities of practice. Soon the entire organization recognized the need to share knowledge, and the Corporate Knowledge Management and Information Access Group was formed to formalize the organizationwide discovery, creation, and diffusion of intellectual capital to accomplish National Semiconductor's business objectives.

The structure that works best for your organization will be determined by what you hope to accomplish and the resources you have to dedicate to your initiatives.

ROLES AND RESPONSIBILITIES

As knowledge management and transfer initiatives grow within an organization, so too do the roles and responsibilities of those involved in the process (Figure 5). Managing knowledge effectively, especially large quantities of it, requires that people be specifically assigned to every stage of the process—including collecting, organizing, adding value, disseminating, and supporting its use.

**People in
Knowledge Management**

Creating Knowledge	Knowledge Management Infrastructure	Applying Knowledge
• Publishers • Network Members • Analysts • External Sources	• Publishing Coordinators • Knowledge Organizers and Architects • Knowledge Managers • Staff in Networks • Help Desks (full-time) • Information Technology • Communication Infrastructure	• Individuals • Networks (led by full-time knowledge managers) • Teams

Figure 5

Leaders and Champions

Strong leadership and sponsorship, especially at the executive level, is necessary for the success of a major knowledge management initiative. While small projects, created at the grassroots level, may succeed without senior management involvement, substantial funding and organizational change require involvement of your firm's executives. Senior leaders also must be tied to an initiative if it has any chance of being linked to the greater organizational strategy.

The top-ranking officials of several companies APQC has studied are zealots about the value of knowledge and sharing best practices. Not surprisingly, it is in these companies especially that knowledge management initiatives have flourished. For instance, knowledge management at The World Bank began to take root only after its president, James Wolfensohn, announced in late 1996 that it would be a key strategy for the organization in its mission to reduce poverty and increase quality of life in developing countries around the world. Since that time, The World Bank—which provides not only loans but also advice and customized resources—has developed a knowledge management system that captures and organizes knowledge, making it accessible to its staff members and clients.

Aside from a highly involved CEO, the most prominent player in a knowledge management initiative is the champion. We learned in our second knowledge management study that champions seem to be located at both the corporate and the business unit levels, rather than predominantly in one or the other. Champions develop the shared vision and provide coordination, facilitation, and encouragement. They often also are responsible for partnering with their information technology colleagues to adapt the most appropriate IT solutions for the initiative.

For instance, Robert Hiebeler, partner for Arthur Andersen's KnowledgeSpace™, works closely with the firm's CIO to ensure that staff members get the best content, delivered by the best IT systems.

Champions can be found at any level of the organization. Generally the more people you have in the champion role, the more energy your knowledge initiative has and the more widespread the impact it can have. Champions can be a major key to success, especially with grassroots initiatives that have yet to gain the attention and support of senior management.

Knowledge Workers

Underneath the champion are the people who make it happen—those who gather, edit, categorize, and distribute the knowledge. For instance, at consulting firm Arthur Andersen, knowledge managers in the Arthur Andersen Sharing Network monitor the knowledge or divergent traffic for 80 sharing communities. They

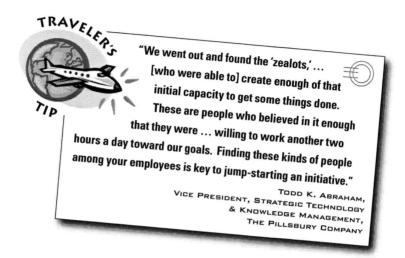

TRAVELER'S TIP

"We went out and found the 'zealots,' ... [who were able to] create enough of that initial capacity to get some things done. These are people who believed in it enough that they were ... willing to work another two hours a day toward our goals. Finding these kinds of people among your employees is key to jump-starting an initiative."

TODD K. ABRAHAM,
VICE PRESIDENT, STRATEGIC TECHNOLOGY
& KNOWLEDGE MANAGEMENT,
THE PILLSBURY COMPANY

identify pieces of information that have high value and then move into the convergent process, where that high-value knowledge is packaged for use.

Staffing service Manpower Inc.'s global account managers are the key link between the success stories and lessons learned of client engagements and the company's Virtual Account Management (VAM) system. The global account managers gather the stories and data to populate VAM, and a staff of writers maintains the information. Having this knowledge accessible and organized helps Manpower better serve its clients.

How many people your organization will have in supporting roles such as these will depend on many factors, including the scope of your initiative, the size of your organization, and the budget allocated to managing or transferring knowledge. Individuals' job titles and responsibilities will vary as well.

Non-Knowledge-Specific Employees

Depending on how extensive your knowledge management plan is, even employees without specific knowledge-related roles may be involved in daily knowledge activities. In fact, knowledge management guru Tom Davenport told attendees at APQC's 1998 knowledge symposium that the "amateurs," not the knowledge professionals, are the ones organizations must depend on to make knowledge management successful. These amateurs—ranging from marketing planners to financial analysts to shop-floor supervisors—are the people who need knowledge to do jobs effectively on a daily basis.

At chemical company Buckman Laboratories, for instance, employees on the front line are expected to use the company's knowledge to serve the customer well, generate cash flow for the organization, and help it expand and flourish. For this to happen, these employees need to be connected, whether in person or through information technology, to the knowledge. Allowing everyone in the organization direct access to knowledge has numerous benefits, among them increasing individuals' value and reducing the distortion of knowledge that naturally occurs as information passes down the line from person to person.

COLLABORATION STRUCTURES

At least as important as the explicit structures for sharing knowledge in an organization are the tacit systems that transfer experiential knowledge and other knowledge that is not easy to write down. Chief among these tacit systems are communities of practice or human networks. Whether formal or informal, these common structures in best-practice organizations enable people with common interests to effectively share knowledge. Most often, such networks are mainly forums for sharing knowledge, rather than for organizing, managing, or maintaining information. People in these groups may meet in a physical space, if their location permits it, or they may have virtual gatherings, using information technology to communicate their ideas.

Jim Tighe, manager of corporate quality at Chevron Corporation, a petroleum and chemical company, has identified the following characteristics common to his company's 100-plus knowledge-sharing communities:

- Members are typically functional counterparts from various parts of the organization. The more value they see in their involvement, the more they tend to participate.
- Purposes range from sharing best practices and lessons learned to improving the individual and collective subject matter expertise of the group.
- Typical methods of interaction include face-to-face meetings, group e-mail, Web sites, Lotus Notes, and conferences and workshops.

In general, communities of practice tend to be self-led and often work out their purpose and methods of communicating, such as those mentioned above, by themselves.

The virtual aspect of communities of practice has made them a natural means of sharing information within another large organization, The World Bank. In fact, 130 communities of practice have emerged within the bank's global environment during the past two years. The organization discovered it had some communities operating informally, so it made them official and allocated funds to support and promote their growth. This formal support is the bank's way of saying, "This is part of how we work here."

ROADBLOCKS TO SUCCESS

- Senior leadership is unwilling to "walk the talk"
- No common process vocabulary
- Lack of teams and teaming approaches
- No ownership of knowledge and learning
- "Silo" mentality
- No formal knowledge transfer process

Most of the best-practice organizations in our 1999 Creating a Knowledge-Sharing Culture study made no effort to formalize their human networks or communities. They did, however, enable these communities to thrive by giving them a budget, information systems, space, library support, time for networking coordinators to manage network-related affairs, and recognition for their contribution.

No matter how your organization decides to structure its sharing communities, or whether they "structure themselves" as they grow from grassroots initiatives, they are an integral part of getting tacit and explicit knowledge from one individual to another.

 **CHECK YOUR STATUS**

1. Who are the primary champions of knowledge management in your organization?

2. What do senior leaders do to champion knowledge management?

3. What roles do people in your organization play that support your knowledge-sharing efforts?

4. How much assistance and intervention do people in your organization need to make transfers happen and get results in a timely manner?

5. How does the infrastructure address problems with the flow and implementation of knowledge?

6. Does your organization have human network systems that support all aspects of knowledge management (e.g., capturing, sharing, and transfering)?

7. Does your organization use designated people, such as facilitators or internal consultants, to support knowledge management initiatives?

8. How widely known and publicized are these human networks and designated people within the organization?

Information Technology

While communicating through technology is by no means new, the pervasive use of groupware and Internet/intranet/extranet technologies has had a profound effect on people's ability to share knowledge and practices effectively. Likewise, people play a major role in such technology's success—if they don't use it, it serves no purpose. Technology is necessary, but not sufficient, to make knowledge transfer happen. Your goal should be "Build it so they will come."

RULES OF THUMB

If you are going to be successful, you need the technology in place; it's got to be good and it's got to be easy to use. However, as Tom Davenport says, "If you are spending more than one-third of your energy and money on the technology side, you're probably not going to be successful."

Ultimately, knowledge and best practices are in people's heads. The behavioral aspects of the system are therefore more important than its architecture. Davenport uses the "stay under one-third of resources" litmus test to ensure IT does not become "the be all and end all" of knowledge management. We offer two other helpful rules of thumb:

- The more "valuable" the knowledge, the less sophisticated the technology that supports it. Here's how it works: Databases and data mining tools, for example, are high on the technological sophistication scale. They contain data. In contrast, help desks, equipped with nothing more than humans and telephones, are low-tech but offer high knowledge value.
- Tacit knowledge is best shared through people; explicit knowledge can be shared through machines. In other words, the more tacit the knowledge, the less high-tech the solution.

KNOWLEDGE-ENABLED INTRANETS

You have to start with an enterprisewide IT platform. Most companies today have already figured out their basic information technology architecture and are building intranets, through which they offer a variety of information and knowledge (Figure 6). To help ensure your intranet-based knowledge management solution achieves its purpose, adhere to the following guidelines:

- Understand the business purpose for what you are trying to accomplish—define the objectives.
- Determine whether the current technology can be adapted or new technology can be purchased off the shelf.
- Assess the ability of the physical infrastructure currently in place to handle the kind and quantity of traffic moving around on the intranet.
- Identify internal support requirements for maintenance of the system.
- Organize your content; you may need librarians.
- Choose a central location for your knowledge management portal or Web site, from which one can navigate to any other area. Think about issues surrounding policies and procedures, training, and redundancies in processes and information.
- Design for ease of use—intranet and Web-based solutions are almost training-free in terms of the technology.

Information Available Through Intranets

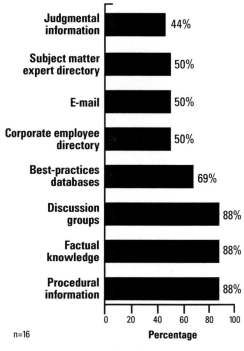

Figure 6

- Facilitate universal access and universal use.
- Consider initial costs, including shareware and software, as well as secondary costs, which can include training, operations and management, increased bandwidth installations, lost productivity due to obsessive use of Web content-creation tools, and fruitless forays into Web junkyards.
- Buy the best search/indexing tool you can afford.
- Have a process in place for putting in, taking out, and "forgetting" knowledge, or deleting information that is obsolete.

Tricon Global Restaurants, which comprises Taco Bell, Kentucky Fried Chicken, and Pizza Hut, has 10,000 corporate employees

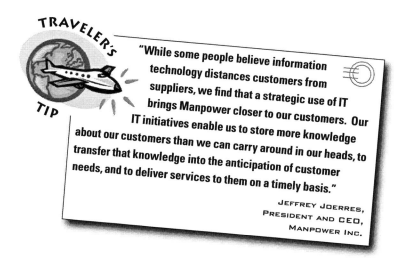

TRAVELER'S

TIP

"While some people believe information technology distances customers from suppliers, we find that a strategic use of IT brings Manpower closer to our customers. Our IT initiatives enable us to store more knowledge about our customers than we can carry around in our heads, to transfer that knowledge into the anticipation of customer needs, and to deliver services to them on a timely basis."

JEFFREY JOERRES,
PRESIDENT AND CEO,
MANPOWER INC.

around the globe and therefore significant opportunties for using intranets as its foundation for knowledge sharing. When Tricon spun off from Pepsico in October 1997, it faced the issue of how to share brand and company information across the three functional silos that made up the new organization. As a result, the company created three separate intranet sites, one for each restaurant chain, that maintained the essence of the brand personalities and harvested the vital information each organization already was creating in Word, PowerPoint, Excel, and other technologies. The company also created the "Triconnection" site, which presents common processes and shared services all three organizations can capitalize on.

At Buckman Laboratories, Web-based forums and the global infrastructure provided by CompuServe have allowed associates to access project tracking systems, customer relationship management systems, groupware, bulletin boards, virtual conference rooms, and databases that capture institutional memory 24 hours a day. K'Netix®—The Buckman Knowledge Network—is the interconnected system of knowledge bases used as a worldwide resource by Buckman Laboratories associates in more than 80 countries. Through it, they can share knowledge electronically—and then pass it on to the customer.

As a global network, K'Netix enables Buckman personnel to collaborate closely, unbounded by factors like distance and time zones. The network encourages open, unrestricted communication among Buckman experts and the free exchange of ideas. This culture is critical in helping Buckman find innovative solutions to customer challenges, as well as develop products in anticipation of future needs.

IT TOOLS AND APPLICATIONS

The following is a brief overview of some of the IT applications being used to support knowledge management and transfer.

1. Structured document repositories (a.k.a. databases)

Structured document repositories typically contain regular, alphanumeric data capable of being stored in conventional relational databases. Best-practice databases are a good example. Another is Web sites with key documents. Best-practice databases are usually repositories of short descriptions of best practices and/or pointers to contacts within the organization who have knowledge about these practices.

Databases that are organized around customers—which may include information about customer inquiries, needs, and interactions—and databases containing competitor intelligence are also examples of what is stored in these repositories. These databases typically include sales presentations, reports, engagement information, competitor analysis, and external feeds.

Consider the following tips when implementing structured document repositories:

- It is important to supply "magnet content" that causes people to use the database in the context of their work.
- Desirable systems automatically capture content rather than require people to take an extra step to re-enter it.
- Every system needs a disciplined process for creation, evaluation, categorization, maintenance, and forgetting—i.e., people have to be assigned these responsibilities.

- Give people a reason to use the database frequently, and make it easy to do so.
- Watch search engine traffic to understand what users are looking for most frequently.

2. Discussion databases

These are discussion groups of project or work teams (whether e-mail bulletin boards, news groups, or Lotus Notes-based forums). They may also support communities of practice, project work teams, and salespeople or sales and marketing teams. Helpful implementation tips include:

- Make sure you have shared norms for participation.
- Provide some payback for participation (tangible or intangible).
- Ensure active facilitation.
- Offer a "one-stop" solution for e-mail and discussion.
- Nourish the online community through other means as well (e.g., face-to-face meetings).
- Remember that content has to be good if the discussion databases are to attract visitors.
- Use logical, intuitive structure for views.
- Use library scientists who understand the technology and technologists who understand library science.
- Provide some editorial and publishing support to increase value and accuracy.
- Capture metadata as well as content.
- Create automatic systems for "cleaning out the closet."

3. Directories of expertise

Before today's search engines were available, companies often used pointer system applications, such as directories of internal experts, project managers, or interested parties that were fed by the corporate HR system. While some organizations still do this, others have begun to ask the employees themselves to maintain their

ROADBLOCKS TO SUCCESS

- Lack of great content
- Lack of common platforms
- Building the IT system first
- Complicated technology—takes more than three "clicks" to find knowledge
- "Localized" technology solutions

expertise information, using whatever terms are most appropriate. Free-text search capabilities make it easy for others to find these experts. The incentive for employees to keep their information up to date is knowing that others will use it to solicit them for internal projects and jobs.

Keep in mind the following when creating directories of experts:

- Maps of experts and communities of practice are at times out of date but are still worthwhile.
- Don't create a pointer system that's basically an electronic version of a phone book. Add value by interconnecting the directory with other components of the knowledge management application suite, so that users can use "hot links" to further refine their needs.
- Experts must be motivated to supply their profiles (market economy).
- "Expert" may be a highly political concept. Communities of practice may be used to help qualify expertise.

4. Transferring via document exchange and video infrastructure

E-mail is the most pervasive and effective means of electronic communication and collaboration. It is real-time, fast, easy, and user-driven. Videoconferencing from the desktop is growing but not ubiquitous like e-mail. Although e-mail is a rich source of information, there is too much of it and it is unfiltered—thus, gems are frequently lost. The creation of public folders for e-mail that contains information that may interest others or the use of collaborative technology for threaded conversations for communities of practice helps ensure that valuable knowledge is shared.

 **CHECK YOUR STATUS**

1. Is the technology group supporting your knowledge management initiatives?
2. Does your organization have an information technology model that supports your knowledge management initiatives?
3. Who are the users of your system?
4. Does your technology link all employees of the organization to one another and to all relevant internal and external data and information?
5. Does your organization have common IT platforms, navigation tools, and protocols?
6. What technology platform will have the greatest ease of use and scalability for the future?
7. Are off-the-shelf applications available?
8. Are IT users provided a standard process taxonomy for sharing and transferring knowledge and best practices?
9. How do people contribute to and use the system?
10. Who is responsible for monitoring the inputs to your system?

Approaches

N ow that we understand the reasons for knowledge management—the business case—and many of the pieces that make up a well-rounded initiative, it's time to think about putting it into action. As we mentioned in the introduction, knowledge is just information unless people are using it.

While the content of the knowledge and the best practices is important to successful knowledge management, so is the approach taken to move this knowledge throughout the organization. Like a lot of other things in life, transfer of knowledge and best practices just doesn't happen because it makes good sense or because management says it should. Using the right approach(es) is critical to ensuring the success of implementation and change.

CHOOSING YOUR APPROACH

A well-chosen transfer approach will successfully facilitate the flow of know-how and best practices. Regardless of the size and complexity of transfer, these approaches share some basic processes and fall into three general designs:

1. Self-directed,
2. Knowledge services and networks, and
3. Facilitated transfer.

The three approaches can be placed on a continuum of increasing likelihood of identified business results and higher resources/ commitment (Figure 7). The more advanced an organization's knowledge management initiatives, the greater the chances that its transfer approaches will be rich and multidimensional. And the more real value you demonstrate to your organization, the easier it will be to move along the continuum.

Three Approaches to Infrastructure

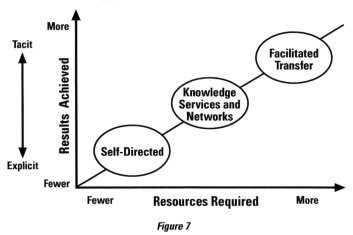

Figure 7

In determining which approach to use, it is important to ask yourself what type of knowledge is being transferred—explicit or tacit. Explicit knowledge (formal/codified) is best transferred through technological solutions, while tacit knowledge (informal/uncodified) is often best transferred via people.

Clearly understanding the type of knowledge to be transferred can help you design the correct transfer approach.

The Self-Directed Transfer Approach

The self-directed approach to a knowledge infrastructure essentially presents people with the technology and then sets them free to use it.

The key component of this approach is the database. No matter the type—e.g., best practices, lessons learned, or project specifics—these databases alone typically do little to transform the information into knowledge. Rather than package the information in ways that help users make sense of it, companies that follow this approach usually leave the deciphering to the user.

This approach, however, often includes pointer systems, ranging from knowledge maps to corporate directories, that simply direct the user to someone who may know more about a particular topic. They don't contain the actual knowledge themselves.

Who: The "knowledge worker"

What: Link person to information

Why: Help people find and access "know-what," "know-who," "know-why," and simple "know-how"
Reduce cycle time, avoid relearning, reduce hassle, free up time for creativity

Where: Right from their desktops

When: In the course of daily work

How: Portals
Search engines
Integrated into process
Shared files/databases
Specific applications

Content:	Explicit knowledge and information
	Databases
	Documents
	Directories and maps to information
	Templates, tools, and presentations
	Computer-based learning
	Performance support systems (case-based reasoning tools)
Critical Success Factors:	Good technology, embedded in work
	Owner for each "object" to ensure quality
	Feedback buttons
	Help desk
	Richness and relevance of information
Risks:	Useless or unreliable information
	Junkyards of abandoned Web pages
	Meager supply of content
	Can't represent the treasure chest of tacit knowledge
	Does nothing to "move information to action"

Chevron's "knowledge map"—located on the company's intranet—includes names, locations, phone numbers, and other pertinent information for people in Chevron worldwide who are working in specified knowledge arenas. This map uses APQC's Process Classification Framework, Malcolm Baldrige National Quality Award criteria, and a key word list to provide ease of access and retrieval for users.

The Knowledge Services and Networks Transfer Approach

"Access to information is important, but access to people with knowledge is more important" is perhaps the best way to characterize this approach. This approach provides, in addition to self-directed components, a variety of knowledge management services and organized networks to assist in the transfer process. People, such as knowledge managers, add value by scanning the flow of information and organizing knowledge into a more usable format.

This approach also involves networks of people, sometimes known as communities of practice or interest, who share with and learn from one another in person and electronically. More information about these groups is found in the Structure and Roles/Responsibilities chapter.

Who:	Groups of people: teams, communities of practice, business functions
What:	Link people by creating a shared space and context for dialogue, advice, and work
Why:	Build relationships Tacit knowledge transfer Project work (across time and space) Speed up learning Speed up action and fast response Build new knowledge "All of us know more than one of us"
How:	Meetings, co-location Group systems—cyber-teams Facilitation and coordination Internet chat and Web collaboration Teleconferencing Videoconferencing
Rewards:	Authorship, peer review Recognition Help
Content:	Work of project teams Peer information exchange New product ideas Support networks of experts and mentors Technical tips

TRAVELER'S TIP

"The glue that holds learning communities together is the personal value proposition. To sustain the involvement a learning community needs, you must provide activities that exceed the value of others. Another key to successful learning community development is setting the appropriate dynamics or environment for sharing, which requires the right balance between facilitation and knowledge brokering."

MICHAEL MAHAFFIE,
TEAM LEADER, KNOWLEDGE MANAGEMENT,
SHELL DEEPWATER DEVELOPMENT INC.

Critical Success Factors:
Shared space and community
Common purpose
Compelling need
Strong coordinators and moderators
Content experts providing perspective, meaning
Norms and expectations

Risks:
Not enough people in the network
Not all people know how or want to work and interact this way
Not a substitute for face-to-face interaction—often increases meetings

Sequent Computer Systems' Sequent Corporate Electronic Library (SCEL) works on a publisher/consumer relationship. Every employee who uses SCEL is a publisher and/or a consumer. Sequent relies on publishers to put knowledge into the system and consumers to use that knowledge.

Publishing coordinators representing functional or business communities in Sequent enter information from their community into the SCEL system so it is available to others. Two librarians help organize the information and help users search for what they need. In addition, there is a SCEL team that monitors the inputs to and outputs from the system.

The Facilitated Transfer Approach

The third approach to knowledge transfer can be considered "full service." Its foundation is the realization that "just because knowledge and best-practice information is available does not mean that action will follow."

This approach provides all of the previous activities and services, plus it designates specific people to stimulate, encourage, and help with the transfer of knowledge and best practices, and often even assist in implementation.

The facilitated transfer approach is the most costly to design but will yield the biggest payoff. As such, an organization using this approach must be confident that the knowledge and best practices are worth the effort to transfer.

ROADBLOCKS TO SUCCESS

- No assessment of current state
- Failure to reuse transfer approaches
- Lack of scaling up a local approach (one-shot approach)
- Not enough tacit knowledge exchange early on
- Transfer approach doesn't achieve results and requires more resources
- Transfer approach adds multiple steps to process

Who:	Unit to unit
What:	Transfer of a successfully demonstrated, complex practice with high return on investment
Why:	Actually transfer the process Close gaps Raise performance Avoid trial and error Shorten the learning curve
How:	Best-practice teams Facilitator network Incorporate new practices into procedures and training systems Interview/knowledge solicitation
Content:	Any process or practice with high impact and gap closure Focus of impact: operations, customer relationship management, products, people/HR, suppliers
Critical Success Factors:	Compelling need or pressure Extensive time and resources Robust methodology Process experts Change management Boundary-spanning authority Ability to transfer people
Risks:	Redeployment of less-than-full-time resources away from knowledge management Limited involvement of the masses due to centralization of facilitators Lack of trust in facilitators' expertise or abilities

American Management Systems uses knowledge associates (facilitators) to connect best practices with people and populate its database. These knowledge associates are chosen because they are leaders in the organization and agree to make tangible contributions to the company's intellectual capital. A team of professional librarians helps catalog all of the contributions and index them for cross-referencing by all AMS employees.

In addition to sharing their knowledge through these contributions on the company intranet, the associates offer their expertise through tools such as e-mail, voice mail, and virtual discussion databases that facilitate expedient communication.

THERE IS NO SINGLE RIGHT APPROACH

The three design approaches discussed in this chapter are steps leading to a multidimensional solution along which organizations choose the mix of activities. Which is best? Each organization has to balance the answers to key transfer questions with its resources, its strategy, and its belief in the importance of knowledge and best practices transfer in the years ahead.

CHECK YOUR STATUS

1. How important is knowledge management to your organizational strategy?

2. What is the nature of the content (information or knowledge) that will be involved?

3. Who will be using the content or participating in the process?

4. How does the process or content fit the way they work?

5. How will the content be captured and refreshed?

6. What methods will be employed to close communication, technical, and tacit/experiential gaps between sources and recipients?

7. What barriers in your organization hinder the transfer of knowledge and best practices?

8. Which approach(es) will address these barriers?

9. What operational improvements will be achieved by using these approaches?

10. What will be the external benefits (customer and market reaction) of using these approaches?

11. What will be the bottom-line benefits gained by using these approaches?

Measurement

I f you don't track and measure your knowledge management activities and results, you will have a hard time understanding what is working (or what is not) and what the payoffs are.

What you measure depends on your purpose.

- If you want to know whether knowledge transfer efforts are achieving their objectives, identify the business results that match your original value proposition and measure those.
- If you want to know which of your knowledge transfer tools and applications are the most effective for sharing practices and know-how, measure the level of transfer activity and ask users how it has helped them achieve business objectives. Look for activity measures and success stories.

A PRACTICAL APPROACH TO MEASUREMENT

Practitioners tell us it is most important to measure the success of the projects and business processes that are being improved through the transfer of knowledge and best practices. Hence, they attempt to link the outcomes of these efforts to their original value proposition. Each comes with its own set of "process," and even financial, measures (see Frequently Used Measures). We therefore believe in measuring processes, activities, and operational outcomes.

Most firms are using some combination of "yardsticks" to gauge the success of their knowledge management projects. In fact, most can clearly describe business improvement outcomes in projects and processes in which knowledge management approaches and applications were used. During our Using Information Technology to Support Knowledge Management benchmarking study, participants indicated the most common business improvement outcomes realized were process improvement and cycle-time reduction, business growth, and employee and customer satisfaction (Figure 8).

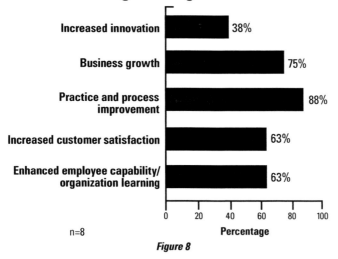

Outcomes Realized as a Result of Knowledge Management Practice

Figure 8

FREQUENTLY USED MEASURES

When measuring the impact of transfer efforts, take into account your original goal. Each value proposition comes with a set of logical "measures" that help monitor your progress toward that goal. These include the following:

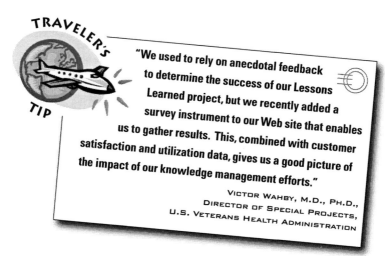

TRAVELER'S TIP

"We used to rely on anecdotal feedback to determine the success of our Lessons Learned project, but we recently added a survey instrument to our Web site that enables us to gather results. This, combined with customer satisfaction and utilization data, gives us a good picture of the impact of our knowledge management efforts."

VICTOR WAHBY, M.D., PH.D.,
DIRECTOR OF SPECIAL PROJECTS,
U.S. VETERANS HEALTH ADMINISTRATION

Customer Intimacy

- Number of customers
- Customer retention rates
- Number of calls handled per day
- Number of calls resolved in the first "sitting"
- Cross-selling penetration
- Revenue from existing customers

Product Leadership

- Revenue from commercialization of new products
- Percentage of revenue from new products
- Time-to-market cycles
- Ratio of successful to not-successful product launches
- Number of launches per year

Operational Excellence

- Cost per unit
- Productivity and yields
- Number of defects/poor quality
- Production cycle time
- Inventory carrying costs

- Environmental compliance
- Safety records

TYPES OF MEASURES: OUTCOMES AND ACTIVITIES

There are two general types of measures that can be used to evaluate knowledge management and transfer activities:

1. *Results:* the measurable (against a benchmark or in dollar terms) impact of the initiative on the outcomes of the projects or processes targeted for improvement, and
2. *Activities:* usage and participation rates of the databases and other knowledge management- and transfer-enabling technologies and tools.

Measuring Results

Since most of the companies with which we work report that their knowledge management efforts are tightly linked to business objectives and business needs, most prefer to measure process and project outcomes.

A good example of measuring business results is Buckman's global measure of sales from new products. Companies like Buckman Laboratories have implemented enterprisewide systems to support the sharing of knowledge and practices, especially in the sales and marketing arena. One of the value propositions behind the K'Netix knowledge-sharing communication system was improving product commercialization by linking salespeople to customers and R&D. To measure how successful its efforts have been, Buckman examines the percentage of sales generated from new products (less than 5 years old). The results speak for themselves:

- 1988–1992 (prior to K'Netix): 23.6 percent
- 1992–1996: 33.3 percent

Other outcomes are as follows:

- Sales per salesperson is up 51 percent.
- Sales per associate is up 34 percent.
- Operating profit per associate is up 93 percent.
- The speed of response to customers is hours, not days or weeks.
- The quality of response has risen all over the world.
- Growth of talented people has increased, since more employees are immersed in high-intensity projects.
- The role of managers is not to manage the flow of information up and down the organization, but to close the gaps.

In the end, Buckman believes it is impossible to put a monetary value on the knowledge network; it is more a basis for the way the company operates.

Measuring Activities

This second group of measures addresses how frequently users are accessing, contributing to, or drawing on the information technology tools that enable knowledge transfer enterprisewide.

There is value in these activity measures. They can lead to a greater understanding of how, or if, a tool or support system of the knowledge management activity is being used. *A caution:* Whereas activity-based measures provide useful information on accessibility, utilization, content quality, and design features, they do not provide information about the impact of these activities on results.

Common activity measures include:

- user rating of effectiveness,
- number of hits,
- participation rates,
- frequency of contribution, and
- frequency of use.

Ultimately, to gain a comprehensive view of the success of knowledge management and transfer efforts, firms rely on the combination package of outcomes and activity measures.

MEASURING KNOWLEDGE MANAGEMENT COSTS

The actual cost of knowledge management and transfer projects is notoriously hard to pin down. Because costs are often dispersed throughout the organization, they can "hide" in places like IT, marketing, HR, and training, as well as in elusive increases in management time and the role of knowledge managers.

However, since there are costs associated with developing support systems, it helps to measure the costs. Here are two examples of knowledge management cost measures:

1. At Sequent Computer Systems, the total spending on knowledge management infrastructure (people and technology) is about $1,000 per employee per year, including all direct costs and some portion of the indirect costs.

2. Buckman spends about 3.75 percent of revenue on knowledge management and transfer activities, including all information technology. Hence, the cost per employee is about $7,500 per year for hardware, software, telephone, network, and staff support.

Knowledge Management People Support Costs

Obviously, the range is quite broad. The difference in per-employee charges reflects more accounting (what gets counted as knowledge management direct expense) than effort. These support costs include:

- facilitating the formation and health of communities of practice and discussion groups,
- populating best-practice databases,
- creating information technology standards for format and information and document management,

ROADBLOCKS TO SUCCESS

- Activities, not results, are measured
- Lack of anecdotal exchange of knowledge
- Measures do not reflect the value proposition
- Failure to capture and publicize "success stories"

- advertising the existence of groups and experts, and
- developing policies and procedures for appropriate use of information and dialogue.

THE COST OF NOT KNOWING (CONK)

There are lots of examples where information and knowledge were somewhere in the organization, but not where they needed to be to avoid a disaster. These examples sometimes become legendary; they are certainly burned into management's memory. When the Challenger space shuttle exploded, some engineers in NASA knew the O-rings in the solid rocket boosters wouldn't hold at low temperatures. But the people who made the decision to launch did not. In a less tragic context, a company launches a new service in China, but the new team doesn't build on experience in that market and makes all the same mistakes again. Sometimes, the cost of not managing knowledge is easier to pinpoint than the positive contribution of effective management. Easier—but can you afford it?

DECIDING WHEN TO MEASURE

To decide when to measure, consider which school of thought applies to your organization: One believes it is premature to measure knowledge management at the beginning because not enough is yet known about the dynamics and impact of knowledge to justify elaborate measurement systems. This school believes measurement at this stage can be risky and misleading. The second school believes that measurement is important for both understanding and legitimizing investment. It wants to know where and how to invest.

We believe you stand the best chance for successful measurement in the early stages of a knowledge management initiative if you focus on the behaviors and attitudes so you can observe, monitor, and nurture. Later on in the initiative you can concentrate on elaborate knowledge management-unique measurement schemes.

CONCLUSION

Ultimately, knowledge about your knowledge management initiatives is important because it helps you:

- design future systems and applications,
- improve the current sharing processes, and
- ensure the effort stays on track (that is, delivers the value proposition!).

Plus, as the role of knowledge managers within organizations grows, such measures will provide the underpinning of their performance evaluation and, hence, compensation.

If you cannot measure it, can you manage it? We don't think so.

CHECK YOUR STATUS

1 Do your organization's knowledge management measures tie back to the organizational strategy and the value proposition?

2. Which knowledge management tools and applications are the most effective for sharing best practices and knowledge?

3. Are you measuring the activities (level of use) of your knowledge management initiatives?

4. What activity measures are you using?

5. How are your activity measures helping you improve your knowledge management initiatives?

6. Are you measuring the process and project outcomes (results) of your knowledge management initiatives?

7 Do your outcomes and business results match your value proposition?

8. Does your measurement system capture anecdotal, or qualitative, measures?

9. Does your organization measure the cost of its knowledge management support systems?

10. Have you captured and publicized successes?

Where Do You Go From Here?

By now you should have a good understanding of where you are related to knowledge management, as well as where you want to be and which landmarks to focus on to get there. But deciding where and how to begin still may be overwhelming.

Whether you choose to start small or to begin with a sweeping initiative or changes, you need to take the plunge and simply expect to make a few mistakes. You can start off on the right path, however, by creating a broad itinerary for yourself based on the following four steps:

- plan,
- design,
- implement, and
- scale up.

PLAN

By reading this book, you've already begun the planning phase—identifying where you are now makes it easier to plan where you are going. Take into consideration your score on the quiz, your answers to the questions in the Landmark chapters, and any "ahas" that may have occurred to you during your reading.

The next step is to focus on your value proposition. Here are some to-dos for determining that essential part of your knowledge management strategy:

1. *Review your organization's competitive, or business, strategy.* Identify the key processes and "drivers" that affect the success of that strategy.

2. *Understand the current state and potential for improvement.* Determine how knowledge management can improve what you're already doing.

3. *Develop a knowledge management framework.* Create a conceptual model of how knowledge management would help this process or project.

4. *Make realistic choices.* Pick a project, process, or problem that the leadership is committed to improving. Next, describe an approach that shows how knowledge management would help.

DESIGN

The design phase involves determining the scale of your project or initiative and determining what resources—technologies, people, etc.—are required to make this happen. Relying on lessons learned or best practices from others at this stage in the process is always wise. If you don't have access to these within your organization, check outside resources: Benchmark other companies, either on your own or in a consortium like the ones APQC facilitates, or read up on best practices and case studies in your topic area (APQC's Best-Practice Reports, based on the findings from our benchmarking studies, are an excellent resource).

This is the time to decide whether you want to begin by applying knowledge management to a specific project or by constructing an organizationwide architecture. Which one you choose depends on what you've learned in this book and our other research publications and activities about your current status and your organization's readiness to embrace and support the initiative.

A detailed project plan with information such as milestones, resources, budget, and deliverable owners will help keep you on track, no matter your desired end result.

The following should be on your to-do list for the design phase:

1. *Find a champion or sponsor who understands the need and has the clout and resources to devote to supporting knowledge management.* Based on the value proposition and the project(s) identified, it may be obvious who that champion should be.

2. *Set up your infrastructure so that someone, be it the champion or not, has primary responsibility for making knowledge management and sharing happen.* If no one has this designation, the initiative will soon fall by the wayside.

3. *Examine the organizational structure that supports your knowledge management efforts.* Make sure you have the resources you need to meet your goals. These resources should have widespread contact throughout the organization rather than have influence limited to a specific area.

4. *Locate any communities of practice or sharing networks that already exist in your organization.* These structures can be helpful in the implementation phase.

5. *Establish standards for technology; they are the key to scale-up.*

6. *Match the knowledge management system with your knowledge management objectives.* Remember, there is no single right way to design a technology architecture to support knowledge management and transfer. By and large, the more tacit and high-value knowledge transfers often involve pointer systems or help desks. A loose interchange and brainstorming session in the conference room may be more productive than using groupware.

7. *Maintain a pragmatic rather than a perfectionist approach.* Emphasize practicality in knowledge structures, desired behaviors, and technology.

IMPLEMENT

Once you've done your planning and design, you're ready for the action phase of your initiative. To successfully launch the project, you'll have to ensure that the people involved have the proper support they need—be it time, technology, human support, etc. You'll also want to be sure that whatever project or initiative you undertake will demonstrate early, visible results. This will provide the justification your project needs for sustenance and growth.

Again, you'll want to turn to others, either inside or outside your organization, for examples of how they've implemented their own projects and for lessons they've learned. There's no reason to make your own mistakes when you can learn from the successes and failures of others.

The following list of actions will help you in the implementation phase.

1. *Create a structure for classifying knowledge.* This structure specifies the categories and terms for the knowledge in which the organization is interested. It will help people contribute to and use the knowledge system.

2. *Get people to meet face to face at the beginning.* Since early exchanges of knowledge often are heavy on the tacit side, it's helpful to allow those involved to interact, rather than to simply access recorded information of what others know and have learned.

3. *Create an environment that encourages sharing.* This means establishing trust among the participants and giving them a reason to contribute.

4. *Empower people to create and add to the knowledge management system.*

5. *Allay people's fears about losing their competitive edge by sharing, rather than hoarding, what they know.* Measurable results are perhaps the best way to show how everyone benefits.

6. *Remain flexible.* Any knowledge management system or approach must be treated as provisional and temporary since both knowledge and the technology for managing it change rapidly.

7. *If you want to know if your knowledge transfer tools and applications are useful, measure the level of use (activities) and ask users how the tools have helped them achieve business objectives.*

8. *If you want to know whether your knowledge transfer efforts are achieving their objectives, identify the business results that match your original value proposition and measure those.*

9. *Celebrate successes early and often.*

SCALE UP

Once you've demonstrated the success of your initial project, you're ready to take on additional initiatives—or perhaps one substantial project designed to capture and use the knowledge of your whole organization. To do this, you'll want to incorporate all the steps in your implementation phase, but on a larger scale. In addition to the actions listed above, consider doing the following as you expand the influence of your project(s):

1. *Capture success stories and use them to "sell" others on what you're doing.*

2. *Make the whole organization aware of the benefits of sharing knowledge.* If you can't make the process part of people's everyday work, create an event that will draw attention to what you're doing and will jump-start the sharing behavior.

3. *Heavily market your knowledge-sharing applications and ensure they meet users' daily needs.* "If we build it, they will come" works only with substantial attention to marketing.

4. *If training in knowledge management or the knowledge management system is necessary, make sure it's available to everyone.*

CONCLUSION

One of the most important lessons we've learned from all the organizations we've studied over the years is that you can't undertake something of this magnitude on your own. Whether you turn to APQC for help from our advisory services, research services, training, benchmarking studies, or other publications or discover other ways to make the contacts and gather the information you need, don't go it alone! After all, learning from others is what successful knowledge management and sharing are all about.

About APQC

F ounded in 1977, the Houston-based American Productivity &
Quality Center provides the knowledge, training, and methods
that empower businesses and other organizations to maximize their
potential with a focus on productivity, quality, and best practices.
APQC is a nonprofit organization and an internationally recognized
leader in benchmarking and best-practice information, serving its
500-plus members and other customers in all sectors of business,
industry, education, and government.

Over the years APQC has built a distinguished list of achieve-
ments, including providing private-sector input into the first White
House Conference on Productivity and spearheading the 1987
creation of the Malcolm Baldrige National Quality Award, which
we jointly administered for its first three years. In 1992 we created
the International Benchmarking Clearinghouse, a comprehensive
service co-designed with customers to facilitate benchmarking.
Our most recent venture is the APQC Education Initiative, a
special program designed to integrate business best practices into
educational institutions.

Today, APQC continues to work with organizations to improve
productivity and quality by providing the tools, information, and
support they need to discover and implement best practices and
obtain results in dozens of process areas.

For information on the many ways APQC can help meet your
organization's knowledge management and process improvement
needs, call 800-776-9676 (713-681-4020 outside the United States)
or visit our Web site at www.apqc.org. To see additional publications, go to www.store.apqc.org.

Attention to Detail:
A Look at Walt Disney World Parks

Volume 1

Keith Black ~ Author/Graphics
Jacquelyn Damon ~ CoAuthor/Photographer

Table of Contents

THANK YOU!

This book would not have been
possible without the Lord's blessing
and help of some very special people.

Thanks must be given to Jackie for the hundreds
of photographs she has taken over the years at the Walt Disney
World Parks, without which this book would not have been possible,
and her encouragement and support in this endeavor.

Thanks also to my wife, Angie, and daughters, Kristen and Lauren,
for their help in looking over this book numerous times as well as
making that first trip together to Walt Disney World so memorable.
If it was not for that trip I may never have been introduced to the work
of Walt Disney and his Imagineers.

Introduction

Since first visiting Walt Disney World in Orlando, Florida with my wife and two daughters in 2003, I began to try and figure out what makes the parks so enjoyable that we all can not wait to return to experience and explore them more.

After reading through many websites, books, and forums as well as listening to podcasts on the subject of Disney, I was drawn to Walt Disney and his vision to provide a clean, entertaining place for families to have fun together. Walt also had a constant desire to improve his creation. His attention to detail and design of guest interaction with the parks intrigued me. He combined his skill as a cartoonist with the fields of film making, architecture and engineering to create what he called Imagineering. Using this unique mixture enabled Walt to fulfill his vision and immerse families into a world of fantasy and imagination. I soon realized the amount of research and effort that went into the parks at Walt Disney World and the fact that there is so much design and detail put into each of these parks that many people do not even realize. Even worse they do not get to experience them. People that do realize this fact still admit to not having seen it all.

So, I have joined with Jackie Damon, another Disney detail enthusiast who I met on the Be Our Guest Podcast Forums, to bring awareness to the incredible work that Walt Disney and his Imagineers have put into these Disney parks. We hope to accomplish this using photographs taken by Jackie during her many trips to the Walt Disney World parks in Orlando, Florida. We seek to test your memory of details you may have seen while on your past visits to the parks and encourage you to take the time to explore and find even more in future visits! Throughout the book we will add insight and information that we have gathered along the way from numerous books, websites, tours, and especially Cast Members working at the parks.

We will begin by taking a broad look at details in the parks and then zoom in a little closer with each level. Each level will consist of thirty-three images of details we have selected from each of the four Disney parks in Orlando, Florida: The Magic Kingdom Park, The Animal Kingdom Park, EPCOT and Disney's Hollywood Studios.
The levels will be as follows:

LEVEL 1: The Weenie Level
LEVEL 2: The Prop Level
LEVEL 3: The Pixie Dust Level

Alongside each detail we have added a small notation area for your use. Let's look at the following example:

Detail 000:

Park: *Magic Kingdom*

Area: *Hub*

Location: *the castle as*

viewed from the hub

First, list the park the detail is located in.
Next, determine the area it is in. This could be the land, area or section of the park like Fantasyland, Asia, World Showcase or Main Street. Finally, describe the exact location of the detail image.

At the end of each level will be a first and second help in case you get stuck or just want to make sure you are thinking of the right location. The first help will reveal the park location while the second help will give more specifics.

Along the way we will have feature details which will be marked with a flash ✦! These details will contain additional information that we learned about, or noticed, during our visits to the parks at Walt Disney World.

Following the levels will be an Answer Section containing the location of all the Disney park details in this book. Many detail answers will even contain additional information, images and tidbits for you to dwell on.

Also included in this book are a couple of scavenger hunts for you to explore with family and friends on future visits to the parks. So we hope you enjoy this compilation of details while remembering Walt and the Imagineers who created them for you to encounter.

Let's get started and see if you have been paying attention to detail!

Magic Kingdom opened October 1, 1971.
It was to be an improved design from the park in California.
Cinderella's Castle is the park icon.
There are seven themed lands:
  Main Street USA, Adventureland, Frontierland, Liberty Square,
  Fantasyland, Tomorrowland, Mickey's Toontown Fair

E.P.C.O.T. opened October 1, 1982.
(**E**xperimental **P**rototype **C**ommunity **O**f **T**omorrow)
This park focuses on Technology and Culture.
Spaceship Earth is the park icon.
There are two sections:
  Future World and World Showcase

Disney's Hollywood Studios opened May 1, 1989.
Originally the park was named Disney-MGM Studios and
was renamed in January 2008.
The theme is based on show business.
The Sorcerer's Hat is the park icon.
There are six themed areas:
  Hollywood Boulevard, Echo Lake, Streets of America,
  Animation Courtyard, Pixar Place, Sunset Boulevard

Animal Kingdom opened April 22, 1998.
Ihis park is aimed at animal conservation.
The Tree of Life is the park icon.
There are seven themed areas:
    The Oasis, Discovery Island, Camp Minnie-Mickey,
    Africa, Rafiki's Planet Watch, Asia, Dinoland USA

4

The Weenie Level

Walt Disney and his Imagineers have excelled in creating a special setting and atmosphere for the many different lands and areas throughout the parks. Each draws you into a realm of excitement, anticipation and adventure.
Walt had the idea of designing and placing large elements in the parks that would create interest from a distance and draw you towards it, a "weenie" as he called it. In keeping with this theme we will look at thirty-three images of buildings, structures and elements in the parks that may have caught your attention. Have you seen...

Disney Park Details (Level 1)

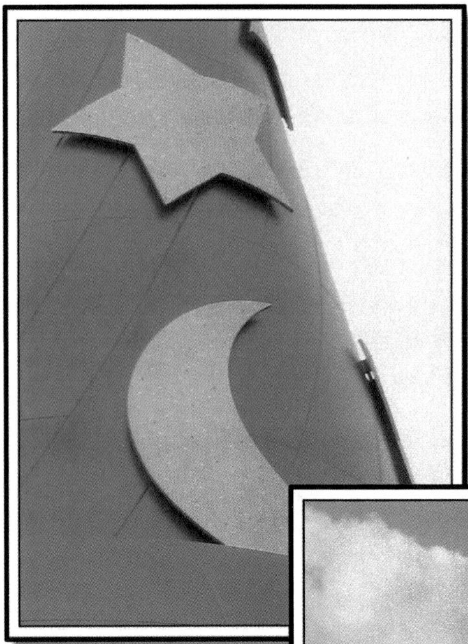

Detail 01:

Park: ____________

Area: ____________

Location: ____________

____

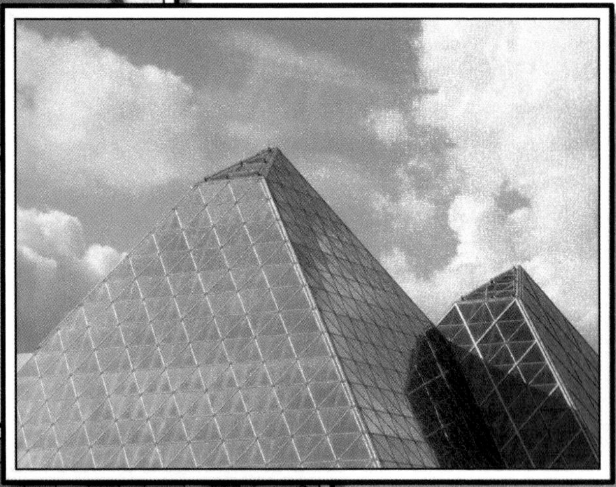

Detail 02:

Park: ____________

Area: ____________

Location: ____________

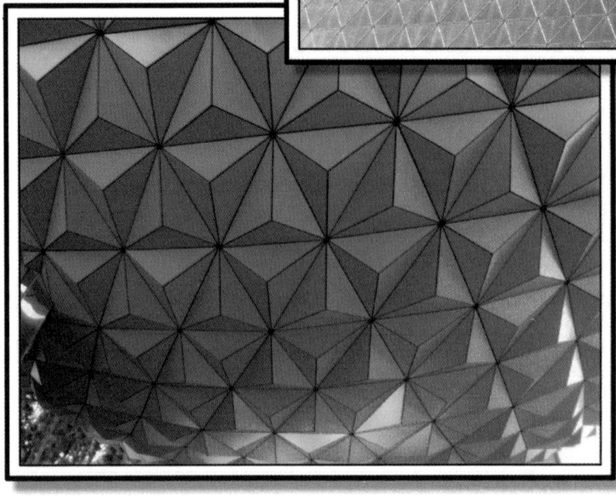

Detail 03:

Park: ____________

Area: ____________

Location: ____________

____

Detail 04:

Park: _____

Area: _____

Location: _____

_____

FEATURED DETAIL:
Did you hear that?

Detail 05:

Park: _____

Area: _____

Location: _____

_____

The research and design put into this structure is not the only Disney detail found here. If you think you hear music and dancing, do not worry because it is coming from the upper story dance and voice lesson studio as listed on the windows!

Detail 06:

Park: _____

Area: _____

Location: _____

_____

Detail 07:

Park: _____

Area: _____

Location: _____

_____

Detail 08:

Park: _____

Area: _____

Location: _____

_____

Detail 09:

Park: _____

Area: _____

Location: _____

_____

Detail 10:

Park: _____

Area: _____

Location: _____

_____

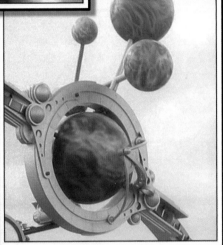

Detail 11:

Park: _____

Area: _____

Location: _____

_____

Detail 12:

Park: _____

Area: _____

Location: _____

_____

FEATURED DETAIL:
This weenie, which serves
as the park icon, is crawling
with details!

Detail 13:

Park: _____

Area: _____

Location: _____

_____

You will be overwhelmed with the amount of detail that artists have
sculpted into this park icon. With a little exploration you will be sure
to find just about every kind of animal you can think of.

Detail 14:

Park: _____

Area: _____

Location: _____

_____

Detail 15:

Park: _____

Area: _____

Location: _____

_____

Detail 16:

Park: _____

Area: _____

Location: _____

_____

Detail 17:

Park: _____

Area: _____

Location: _____

_____

Detail 18:

Park: _____

Area: _____

Location: _____

Detail 19:

Park: _____

Area: _____

Location: _____

_____

Detail 20:

Park: _____

Area: _____

Location: _____

_____

FEATURED DETAIL:
Imagineers paying attention
to the guests' line of sight.

Detail 21:

Park: _____

Area: _____

Location: _____

_____

Using this line of sight as an example, the Imagineers have thought ahead
when it comes to objects seen in the distance that might take away from
the guests' experience in the park they are currently enjoying. Notice the
color and features on the building in the back right of the image. It is not
within this park, but is actually located in an adjacent park. Refer to
the answers page for its name if you do not already know!

Detail 22:

Park: _____

Area: _____

Location: _____

_____

Detail 23:

Park: _____

Area: _____

Location: _____

_____

FEATURED DETAIL:
If you are new to the Disney Parks you may not recognize this building because it has taken a back seat to the latest park icon for this park. When this particular park opened in May of 1989 this building was a focal point for guests as they entered the main gate.

Detail 24:

Park: _____

Area: _____

Location: _____

_____

Detail 25:

Park: _____

Area: _____

Location: _____

Detail 26:

Park: _____

Area: _____

Location: _____

_____

Detail 27:

Park: _____

Area: _____

Location: _____

_____

Detail 28:

Park: _____

Area: _____

Location: _____

Detail 29:

Park: _____

Area: _____

Location: _____

_____

FEATURED DETAIL:
Once you find this relaxing spot amongst beautiful flowers and shrubs you may wonder what it is used for. Well, beyond its current use for private events, this covering of ornate metal detailing once was the loading area for a boat attraction in this park which closed due to the high maintenance cost and upkeep of the boats themselves. Refer to the answers section for the name of the attraction.

Detail 30:

Park: _____

Area: _____

Location: _____

_____

Detail 31:

Park: _____

Area: _____

Location: _____

_____

17

Detail 32:

Park: _____

Area: _____

Location: _____

_____

Detail 33:

Park: _____

Area: _____

Location: _____

_____

FEATURED DETAIL:
Beyond the glass windows seen here is a fairytale in itself! The restaurant inside serves breakfast, lunch and dinner and is full of character. But be sure to make your advanced dining reservations as soon as the 180 day window opens or you might only get to experience it from the perspective shown above.

First Help

The Weenie Level

The park location of each Level 1 Disney Park
Detail image is revealed in this help.

Detail 01: Disney's Hollywood Studios
Detail 02: EPCOT
Detail 03: EPCOT
Detail 04: Disney's Hollywood Studios
Detail 05: Magic Kingdom
Detail 06: Animal Kingdom
Detail 07: Disney's Hollywood Studios
Detail 08: Magic Kingdom
Detail 09: EPCOT
Detail 10: Magic Kingdom
Detail 11: Magic Kingdom
Detail 12: Animal Kingdom
Detail 13: Animal Kingdom
Detail 14: Magic Kingdom
Detail 15: Animal Kingdom
Detail 16: Animal Kingdom
Detail 17: Magic Kingdom
Detail 18: Magic Kingdom
Detail 19: Magic Kingdom
Detail 20: Disney's Hollywood Studios
Detail 21: EPCOT
Detail 22: EPCOT
Detail 23: Disney's Hollywood Studios
Detail 24: EPCOT
Detail 25: Magic Kingdom
Detail 26: EPCOT
Detail 27: Magic Kingdom
Detail 28: Disney's Hollywood Studios
Detail 29: Magic Kingdom
Detail 30: Magic Kingdom
Detail 31: EPCOT
Detail 32: EPCOT
Detail 33: Magic Kingdom

Second Help

The Weenie Level

A more general park location of each Level 1 Disney
Park Detail image is revealed in this help.

Detail 01: Right down Hollywood Boulevard!

Detail 02: You can find these peaks on the west side of Future World.

Detail 03: Can't miss this as you enter EPCOT.

Detail 04: Go past Commissary Lane and take a turn down these streets.

Detail 05: Take a turn off of Main Street and you will find this facade.

Detail 06: Deep in the heart of Asia you can find these snowy peaks.

Detail 07: This ship has dropped anchor just off of Hollywood Boulevard.

Detail 08: Go to Frontierland and look for this mountain!

Detail 09: You will find this Red Planet on the east side of Future World.

Detail 10: Orbiting high above Tomorrowland is this detail.

Detail 11: This is the only mountain in Tomorrowland.

Detail 12: Check out this aged shelter in Dinoland USA.

Detail 13: This park icon is in Discovery Island.

Detail 14: Across the water from Liberty Square is this island rest area.

Detail 15: Seek refreshment at this building found in Asia.

Detail 16: Find this on the outskirts of Asia.

Detail 17: Look up in Adventureland to see this cupola detail.

Detail 18: Go to Town Square to find this Car Barn.

Detail 19: Check out this ironwork in Town Square.

Detail 20: Look beyond the Animation Courtyard.

Detail 21: Find this land in the World Showcase.

Detail 22: This can be found in the World Showcase.

Detail 23: At the end of Hollywood Boulevard near the hat.

Detail 24: Find this architecture in the World Showcase.

Detail 25: Catch a glimpse of this structure from Fantasyland.

Detail 26: Find this stone structure in the World Showcase.

Detail 27: This weather vane is found near Liberty Square.

Detail 28: Go down Sunset Boulevard to search for this structure.

Detail 29: Tasty treats await in this building in Liberty Square.

Detail 30: Find this shady spot near the Hub.

Detail 31: This temple structure is in the World Showcase.

Detail 32: This detailed replica is in the World Showcase.

Detail 33: This view can be found from Fantasyland.

The Prop Level

After being drawn into the parks, Walt and his Imagineers transport you into a world of fantasy and imagination with the proper placement of details that we will refer to as props for this level. These props set the scene and create an atmosphere for the different lands and areas throughout the parks for your enjoyment. Let us look at thirty-three more images that focus on these types of Disney details.
Have you seen...

Detail 34:

Park: _____

Area: _____

Location: _____

_____

Detail 35:

Park: _____

Area: _____

Location: _____

_____

Detail 36:

Park: _____

Area: _____

Location: _____

_____

Detail 37:

Park: _____

Area: _____

Location: _____

_____

FEATURED DETAIL:
Hold that train!

Have you ever ridden
a train at Disney?
Well, if you happen to find this one, climb
aboard! This train will take you on a short
journey to a wild place full of exploration
and learning!

Detail 38:

Park: _____

Area: _____

Location: _____

_____

25

Detail 39:

Park: _____

Area: _____

Location: _____

_____

Detail 40:

Park: _____

Area: _____

Location: _____

Detail 41:

Park: _____

Area: _____

Location: _____

_____

Detail 42:
Park: _____

Area: _____

Location: _____

_____

Detail 43:
Park: _____

Area: _____

Location: _____

Detail 44:
Park: _____

Area: _____

Location: _____

_____

Detail 45:

Park: _____

Area: _____

Location: _____

_____

FEATURED DETAIL:
This tree is loaded with history! Once you have found this tree seek the plaques which give insight about the tree, the hanging lanterns and the history behind it all.

Detail 46:

Park: _____

Area: _____

Location: _____

_____

Detail 47:

Park: _____

Area: _____

Location: _____

_____

Detail 48:

Park: _____

Area: _____

Location: _____

_____

FEATURED DETAIL:
Down to the last detail! If you have ever seen these props set up in this park then you might have also taken a closer look at the actual painting. But if not, you should be paying more attention to detail! The painting is of the scene across the way.

Detail 49:

Park: _____

Area: _____

Location: _____

_____

Detail 50:

Park: _____

Area: _____

Location: _____

Detail 51:

Park: _____

Area: _____

Location: _____

_____

Detail 52:

Park: _____

Area: _____

Location: _____

_____

FEATURED DETAIL:
Imagineers follow through with their attention to detail with not only the props set on the porch in this image but also the railings, posts, light fixtures and complete building. These aesthetics truly give you a feel of a different time and place. Be sure not to breeze through town but take time to soak up your surroundings.

Detail 53:

Park: _____

Area: _____

Location: _____

_____

31

Detail 54:

Park: _____

Area: _____

Location: _____

_____

Detail 55:

Park: _____

Area: _____

Location: _____

Detail 56:

Park: _____

Area: _____

Location: _____

_____

Detail 57:

Park: _____

Area: _____

Location: _____

_____

Detail 58:

Park: _____

Area: _____

Location: _____

_____

FEATURED DETAIL:
Down to the shoe and nail! It is these little additions of detail that add so much depth to your experience of the parks whether you actually notice them or not. When you begin to realize these types of details it opens your eyes to another world.

This particular detail exists at a location that was used for a past attraction that is no longer in commission. Refer to the answers section for the name of the attraction.

Detail 59:

Park: _____

Area: _____

Location: _____

_____

Detail 60:

Park: _____

Area: _____

Location: _____

Detail 61:

Park: _____

Area: _____

Location: _____

_____

Detail 62:

Park: _____

Area: _____

Location: _____

_____

Detail 63:

Park: _____

Area: _____

Location: _____

_____

FEATURED DETAIL:

The addition of actual furniture, stoves, lanterns and toys with an aged look creates an accurate setting for the guests as they wander through this area of country. So next time you are sightseeing be sure to take in the all the details!

Detail 64:

Park: _____

Area: _____

Location: _____

_____

Detail 65:

Park: _____

Area: _____

Location: _____

Detail 66:

Park: _____

Area: _____

Location: _____

_____

First Help

The Prop Level

The park location of each Level 2 Disney Park
Detail image is revealed in this help.

Detail 34: Animal Kingdom
Detail 35: Disney's Hollywood Studios
Detail 36: Disney's Hollywood Studios
Detail 37: Magic Kingdom
Detail 38: Animal Kingdom
Detail 39: Disney's Hollywood Studios
Detail 40: Disney's Hollywood Studios
Detail 41: Animal Kingdom
Detail 42: Disney's Hollywood Studios
Detail 43: Magic Kingdom
Detail 44: Disney's Hollywood Studios
Detail 45: Magic Kingdom
Detail 46: Disney's Hollywood Studios
Detail 47: Disney's Hollywood Studios
Detail 48: EPCOT
Detail 49: Magic Kingdom
Detail 50: Disney's Hollywood Studios
Detail 51: Magic Kingdom
Detail 52: Magic Kingdom
Detail 53: Magic Kingdom
Detail 54: EPCOT
Detail 55: EPCOT
Detail 56: Disney's Hollywood Studios
Detail 57: Magic Kingdom
Detail 58: Magic Kingdom
Detail 59: Animal Kingdom
Detail 60: Magic Kingdom
Detail 61: Magic Kingdom
Detail 62: Magic Kingdom
Detail 63: EPCOT
Detail 64: Disney's Hollywood Studios
Detail 65: EPCOT
Detail 66: Magic Kingdom

Second Help

The Prop Level

A more general park location of each Level 2 Disney Park Detail image is revealed in this help.

Detail 34: Look for these supplies in Africa.

Detail 35: Look for this crash near the Streets of America!

Detail 36: Props galore near Echo Lake.

Detail 37: Snakes! I hate snakes! Find these in Adventureland.

Detail 38: Catch this train in Africa.

Detail 39: Which way do we go from here just inside the park entrance?

Detail 40: This sign is hanging around near Echo Lake.

Detail 41: Find this direction in Dinoland USA.

Detail 42: Look in the Animation Courtyard.

Detail 43: Tomorrowland!

Detail 44: Go along Hollywood Boulevard.

Detail 45: Look in Liberty Square.

Detail 46: "C" "1" store in Pixar Place.

Detail 47: Hiding away in the Echo Lake district.

Detail 48: This artistic expression can be found in the World Showcase.

Detail 49: Between the Land of Fantasy and Tomorrow.

Detail 50: Within Echo Lake.

Detail 51: Search through Fantasyland.

Detail 52: Down in Frontierland.

Detail 53: Look closely in Frontierland.

Detail 54: World Showcase hides this water well.

Detail 55: The World Showcase holds this timepiece.

Detail 56: Rats in the Streets of America!

Detail 57: Look out for this detail in Frontierland.

Detail 58: Good luck finding this detail in Liberty Square.

Detail 59: Look along this Trek in Asia.

Detail 60: A sign that you are entering Adventureland!

Detail 61: Take notice of this planter in Adventureland.

Detail 62: Off the beaten path of the Hub.

Detail 63: The World Showcase harbors these props.

Detail 64: Look for this snow on the Streets of America.

Detail 65: Look for this booth in the World Showcase.

Detail 66: Wait here while I go look in the Briar Patch.

LEVEL 3

The Pixie Dust Level

Finally, you have been drawn in and immersed into the
world of fantasy and imagination that Walt and his
Imagineers have created for you only to discover that the
attention to detail goes even further. If you take the time to
explore, you may be surprised to find that little extra pixie
dust detail which continues the story line and adds to your
enjoyment of the parks. These final thirty-three images
focus on special details that you may never see
unless you begin to pay attention to detail!
Have you seen...

Detail 67:

Park: _____

Area: _____

Location: _____

_____

FEATURED DETAIL:
Everything may not be what it seems at Walt Disney World! Take this trash can for example. It is a mobile and vocal trash can that will draw kids like flies. This detail can be found in a certain area of this park and if you have ever seen it, you know there is always a crowd.

Detail 68:

Park: _____

Area: _____

Location: _____

_____

Detail 69:

Park: _____

Area: _____

Location: _____

_____

Detail 70:

Park: _____

Area: _____

Location: _____

_____

FEATURED DETAIL:
Mine!....Mine! Mine!........Mine!
Imagineers take a simple entrance area and bring life to it, adding
to every guest's enjoyment. This detail will bring a smile to your
face if you have seen the popular animated movie from which
these birds came........Mine!

43

Where

Disney Park Details (Level 3)

Have you ever noticed the ground on which you walk in the parks?

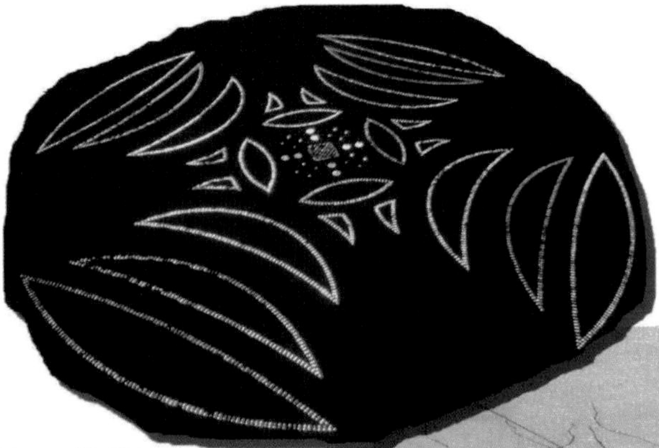

Detail 71:

Park: ______________

Area: ______________

Location: ______________

____

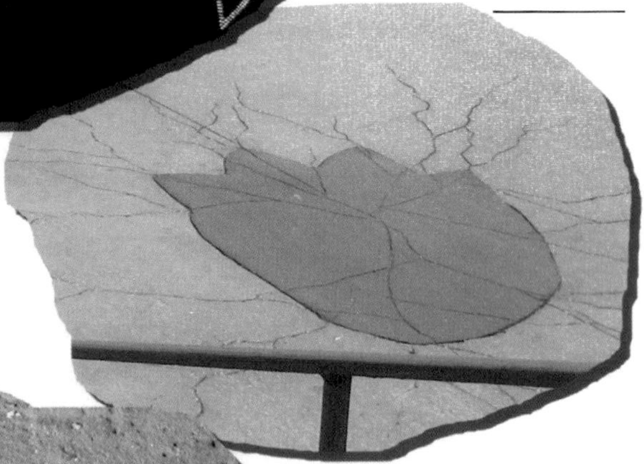

Detail 72:

Park: ______________

Area: ______________

Location: ______________

____

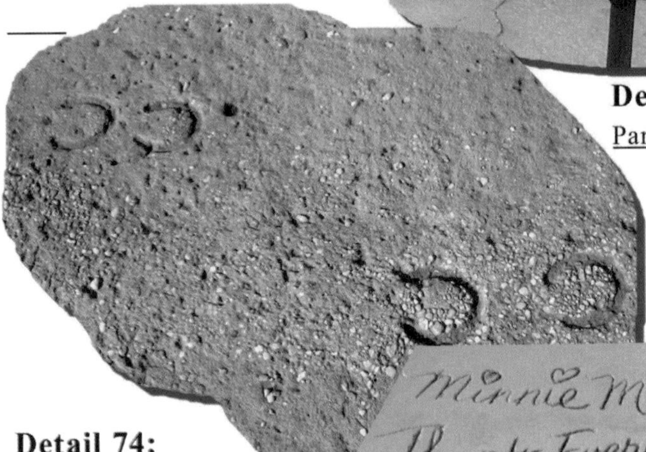

Detail 73:

Park: ______________

Area: ______________

Location: ______________

____

Minnie Mouse
Thanks Everyone
XOXO
5/1/89

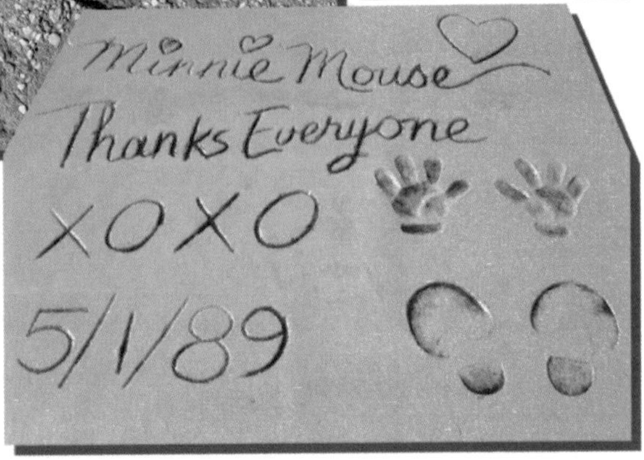

Detail 74:

Park: ______________

Area: ______________

Location: ______________

____

Detail 75:
Park: _____

Area: _____

Location: _____

_____

Detail 76:
Park: _____

Area: _____

Location: _____

_____

Detail 77:
Park: _____

Area: _____

Location: _____

_____

Next time you are in this area, see if you can find a cast member who can tell you the reason behind this pavement flow!

Detail 78:

Park: _____

Area: _____

Location: _____

_____

Detail 79:

Park: _____

Area: _____

Location: _____

_____

Detail 80:

Park: _____

Area: _____

Location: _____

_____

Detail 81:
Park: _____

Area: _____

Location: _____

_____

Detail 82:
Park: _____

Area: _____

Location: _____

_____

Detail 83:
Park: _____

Area: _____

Location: _____

_____

FEATURED DETAIL:
Have you seen this statue of Cinderella and her little friends?

Detail 84:

Park: _____

Area: _____

Location: _____

_____

An added detail to this statue is a continuation of the storyline: If you lean down just enough you can see Cinderella being crowned. This photo shows the proper angle which aligns the statue with the crown on the backdrop which alludes to her future royalty!

Detail 85:

Park: _____

Area: _____

Location: _____

_____

Murals

located throughout the Walt Disney World Parks
continue or add to the storylines of their particular area.
Take time to look at the design and detail put into each of these
works of art.

Detail 86:

Park:_____

Area:_____

Location:_____

_____

Detail 87:

Park:_____

Area:_____

Location:_____

_____

49

Detail 88:

Park: _____

Area: _____

Location: _____

_____

Detail 89:

Park: _____

Area: _____

Location: _____

Detail 90:

Park: _____

Area: _____

Location: _____

_____

Detail 91:

Park: _____

Area: _____

Location: _____

_____

FEATURED DETAIL:
I wonder where that beanstalk goes.
Explore the shop at this location and you will find more details to this tale, including a character who has a giant part in the story!

Detail 92:

Park: _____

Area: _____

Location: _____

_____

FEATURED DETAIL:
This Barber Shop is not just a fitting facade for this area but an actual working shop that anyone can stop in and get a cut.

Detail 93:

Park: _____

Area: _____

Location: _____

_____

FEATURED DETAIL:
This peaceful water way
creates a separation between
two areas of this park as well
as symbolizes a river that
similarly separates areas of
this country!

Detail 94:

Park: _____

Area: _____

Location: _____

_____

Remembrance
There are many details in the parks that give recognition
to those who have contributed to this amazing place.

Detail 95:

Park: _____

Area: _____

Location: _____

_____

Detail 96:

Park: _____

Area: _____

Location: _____

_____

Detail 97:

Park: _____

Area: _____

Location: _____

_____

Detail 98:

Park: _____

Area: _____

Location: _____

_____

FEATURED DETAIL:
Even with the great detail that Imagineers have already put into the parks they continue to amaze guests with park overlays during holiday seasons. Check out the ice over of this popular park icon!

Detail 99:

Park: _____

Area: _____

Location: _____

_____

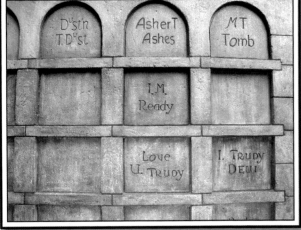

As we close out this book on the Walt Disney World parks we leave you with an image of a detail that is just inside the perimeter of this attraction.

Imagineers have added details to the attractions which add to the guest's enjoyment if they pay attention to detail! Look for our book that focuses on Disney attraction details that will be available soon.

First Help

The Pixie Dust Level

The park location of each Level 3 Disney Park
Detail image is revealed in this help.

Detail 67: Magic Kingdom Park
Detail 68: Disney's Hollywood Studios
Detail 69: Magic Kingdom
Detail 70: EPCOT
Detail 71: EPCOT
Detail 72: Disney's Hollywood Studios
Detail 73: Magic Kingdom
Detail 74: Disney's Hollywood Studios
Detail 75: Magic Kingdom
Detail 76: Magic Kingdom
Detail 77: Magic Kingdom
Detail 78: EPCOT
Detail 79: Magic Kingdom
Detail 80: Animal Kingdom
Detail 81: EPCOT
Detail 82: Magic Kingdom
Detail 83: Animal Kingdom
Detail 84: Magic Kingdom
Detail 85: Disney's Hollywood Studios
Detail 86: Magic Kingdom
Detail 87: EPCOT
Detail 88: Magic Kingdom
Detail 89: Disney's Hollywood Studios
Detail 90: Disney's Hollywood Studios
Detail 91: Magic Kingdom
Detail 92: Magic Kingdom
Detail 93: EPCOT
Detail 94: Magic Kingdom
Detail 95: Magic Kingdom
Detail 96: Disney's Hollywood Studios
Detail 97: Magic Kingdom
Detail 98: Magic Kingdom
Detail 99: Magic Kingdom

Second Help

The Pixie Dust Level

A more general park location of each Level 3 Disney
Park Detail image is revealed in this help.

Detail 67: Search the trash cans in Tomorrowland.

Detail 68: Look around Echo Lake for this detail.

Detail 69: Inside one of the shops on Main Street is this phone.

Detail 70: Listen for "MINE" on the west side of Future World.

Detail 71: Check out this pavement in Future World.

Detail 72: These prints are around Echo Lake.

Detail 73: Find these horseshoe prints in Liberty Square.

Detail 74: Look down Hollywood Boulevard for this walk of fame.

Detail 75: Take a close look around the Town Square.

Detail 76: Search for this treasure in Adventureland.

Detail 77: It's running through Liberty Square.

Detail 78: Search out World Showcase for this background.

Detail 79: Near the Hub lurks this topiary monster!

Detail 80: Focus on Rafiki's Planet Watch.

Detail 81: Check out this building detail in the World Showcase.

Detail 82: Look around the Hub for this detail.

Detail 83: Colorful Buildings! Look in Dinoland USA.

Detail 84: Look around Fantasyland.

Detail 85: Look in the back of the Streets of America area.

Detail 86: Search the castle for this mural.

Detail 87: Look to the west side of Future World for this mural.

Detail 88: Look in Tomorrowland for this Robo Newz.

Detail 89: This FX detail is near the Streets of America.

Detail 90: Search around the Streets of America.

Detail 91: Look around Fantasyland.

Detail 92: Look for the barber pole in Town Square.

Detail 93: This upward waterfall fits this area in Future World.

Detail 94: Search between Liberty Square and Frontierland.

Detail 95: Look up, down the Main Street area.

Detail 96: Off of Echo Lake is this famed area.

Detail 97: Look around Town Square.

Detail 98: During Christmas is when the lights on this icon are visible.

Detail 99: Look just inside this attraction area near Liberty Square.

ANSWERS

The following pages contain answers to the Disney Park Details contained in this book along with additional information and tidbits! So, if you have used all your helps and still do not know where you can find the image or just want to make sure you were correct, go ahead and take a look!

ANSWERS

Detail 01: This is the Sorcerer's Hat located at the end of Hollywood Boulevard in Disney's Hollywood Studios. It serves as the park icon and main weenie which draws guests to the central crossroads of the park. This hat was inspired by the Disney animated film <u>The Sorcerer's Apprentice</u> and replaced the previous park icon, the Earful Tower, in 2001. It also hides the original park weenie, the Grauman's Chinese Theater.

Detail 02: This is the glass mountain range of the Imagination Pavilion found on the west side of Future World in EPCOT and home to the Journey Into Imagination With Figment Attraction.

Detail 03: This is Spaceship Earth, the "Big Golf Ball" as some call it, located at the entrance in EPCOT. This park icon is a complete geodesic sphere reaching eighteen stories in height and containing an attraction by the same name inside.

Detail 04: This is a row of residence facades on Gillespie Street in the Streets of America area in Disney's Hollywood Studios. They are located behind Commissary Lane toward the back of the park. If you are ever down this alley at Christmas time you can see the incredible lighting effects of the Osborne Lights. It has also been said that if you listen closely you can even hear the sounds of busy city streets.

Detail 05: This is a building facade located on Center Street, just off of Main Street in Magic Kingdom. If you look closely at the upper story windows you will see references to a dance & voice lesson studio. From this location you can hear sounds of classes taking place, if the park noise is not too loud.

Detail 06: These are the snowy peaks of the Expedition Everest Attraction in the land of Asia in Animal Kingdom. Imagineers put in many hours of research to bring this attraction to life. During the ride you cross over the tallest peak known as the Forbidden Mountain in an effort to get to Mount Everest (marked by the arrow in

the adjacent image) only to run into some problems along the way!

Detail 07: This is the S.S. Down the Hatch found at the edge of Echo Lake closest to the Sorcerer's Hat in Disney's Hollywood Studios. It serves as a snack location for the main hub of the park.

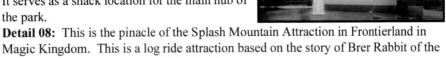

Detail 08: This is the pinacle of the Splash Mountain Attraction in Frontierland in Magic Kingdom. This is a log ride attraction based on the story of Brer Rabbit of the animated Disney classic <u>Song of the South.</u>

Detail 09: This is a close up of the Red Planet at the entrance of the Mission: Space Attraction found on the east side of Future World in EPCOT. This attraction opened in 2003 replacing the former Horizons pavilion.

~ ANSWERS ~

Detail 10: This is a glimpse of the orbiting planets of the Astro Orbiter Attraction in Tomorrowland in Magic Kingdom. This rocket ride is atop Rocket Tower Plaza and is accessed via an elevator found on the side of the plaza closest to the Space Mountain Attraction. This planetary sculpture takes on a whole new feel at night with its illumination!

Detail 11: This is the well known futuristic peak of the Space Mountain Attraction in Tomorrowland in Magic Kingdom. As guests approach the park, the view of this building causes a sense of anticipation of the fun that awaits!

Detail 12: This is a building extension of Restaurantasaurus in Dinoland USA in Animal Kingdom. It takes the form of an old rusted barrack apparently used by paleontologists while digging for dinosaur bones.

Detail 13: This is the Tree Of Life, located in the center of Discovery Island in Animal Kingdom. It is covered with over 320 animal carvings by twenty different artists. Next time you visit this park take the time to explore the wonderful detail found all around the trunk of this tree. This park icon also serves as the home of the It's Tough to be a Bug Attraction, a Disney 4-D show not to be missed!

Detail 14: This is Aunt Polly's Dockside Inn located on Tom Sawyer's Island in Frontierland in Magic Kingdom. This shady spot, as seen from the Liberty Belle Riverboat Dock in Liberty Square, used to serve picnic lunches that you could enjoy in this peaceful setting.

Detail 15: This is a refreshment building found on your left as you cross the bridge from Asia to Discovery Island in Animal Kingdom.

Detail 16: This covered area and dock are located in Asia across from the Flights of Wonder Theatre in Animal Kingdom. It served as one of the loading areas for the Discovery River Boats Attraction (which only stayed in operation about a year after the park opened in 1998).

Detail 17: This is the cupola detail found atop the Zanzibar Trading Company Shop in Adventureland in Magic Kingdom across from the Swiss Family Treehouse Attraction.

Detail 18: This is the Car Barn found in Town Square between the Firehouse and Barber Shop in Magic Kingdom. It is the starting point for the Main Street Vehicles and parades.

Detail 19: This is the park side view of the Train Station in Town Square in Magic Kingdom showing the ironwork detail.

~ ANSWERS ~

Detail 20: This is the Earful Tower, the original park icon for Disney's Hollywood Studios, located on the outskirts of the park behind the buildings in the Animation Courtyard. This 130 foot tall water tower is not a working water tower but was built to add to the characteristics of the studios of old.

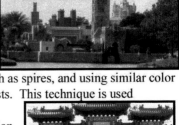

Detail 21: This is the Morocco Pavilion in World Showcase in EPCOT as seen from Future World. The building just to the right (marked with the arrow in the adjacent picture) is the Tower of Terror Attraction in Disney's Hollywood Studios. Imagineers blended the look of this attraction with Morocco by adding architectural features, such as spires, and using similar color tones so as not to distract from the view of the guests. This technique is used throughout the parks.

Detail 22: This is the entryway to the China Pavilion in World Showcase in EPCOT. The amount of detail shown on the entry is carried throughout this pavilion.

Detail 23: This is a scaled replica of the famous Grauman's Chinese Theatre facade in Hollywood, California and is found behind the Sorcerer's Hat on Hollywood Boulevard in Disney's Hollywood Studios. This building served as the original weenie for the park as guests entered.

Detail 24: This is a grouping of buildings on the left side of the Germany Pavilion in World Showcase in EPCOT.

Detail 25: This ornate structure is the old Skyway Station on the hilltop of Fantasyland in Magic Kingdom. It transported guests back and forth to Tomorrowland by gondola lift vehicles. This attraction opened with the park in 1971 and was closed in late 1999.

Detail 26: This is the beautiful stone work of the Akershus Royal Banquet Hall found on the right side of the Norway Pavilion in World Showcase in EPCOT. Within these walls is home to the Princess Storybook Character Dining.

Detail 27: This is the cupola with bat weather vane on the Haunted Mansion in Liberty Square in Magic Kingdom. This place is crawling with spooky details so keep your eyes open while heading through the grounds of this original park attraction!

Detail 28: This is a different angle of the Tower of Terror Attraction at the end of Sunset Boulevard in Disney's Hollywood Studios.

Detail 29: This is the Sleepy Hollow refreshment area on the right just as you enter into Liberty Square in Magic Kingdom. Excellent treats are ready to be had here!

Detail 30: This was the loading area for the Plaza Swan Boats Attraction located just to the right of the hub in Magic Kingdom. It was a picturesque attraction as swan shaped boats glided around the castle moat and through the beautiful grounds. This attraction closed in 1983. The loading area is used as a covering for special events.

Detail 31: This is the step pyramid at the Mexico Pavilion in World Showcase in EPCOT which contains a restaurant, attraction and shopping for your enjoyment all under a star filled evening sky!

Detail 32: This is a replica of Venice's Doge's Palace at the Italy Pavilion in World Showcase in EPCOT. Imagineers draw guests into the pavilion with the beauty of the materials and attention to the detail of the design.

Detail 33: This is Cinderella's Castle as seen from Fantasyland in Magic Kingdom. Within these decorative castle windows you will find Cinderella's Royal Table Restaurant. It serves character meals throughout the day for all little prince and princesses to enjoy.

Detail 34: This is a set of supplies parked along the wall of the river bank near the bridge in Africa before crossing over to Discovery Island in Animal Kingdom.

Detail 35: This is a crash scene at the entrance of the Studio Backlot Tour Attraction back in the Streets of America area in Disney's Hollywood Studios.

Detail 36: This is an arrangement of props in front of the Indiana Jones Epic Stunt Spectacular Attraction in the Echo Lake area in Disney's Hollywood Studios.

Detail 37: This is a snake cart display found outside the entrance to the Zanzibar Trading Company shop near the Magic Carpets of Aladdin Attraction in Adventureland in Magic Kingdom.

Detail 38: This is the Wildlife Express Train which can be caught in Africa in Animal Kingdom near the Pangani Forest Exploration Trail. It transports you to Rafiki's Planet Watch and Conservation Station.

Detail 39: This is a directional sign next to Sid Cahuenga's One-of-a-Kind Shop which is on the left of the entry plaza as you enter Disney's Hollywood Studios.

Detail 40: This is the Tune In Lounge sign which is next to the 50's Prime Time Cafe in the Echo Lake area in Disney's Hollywood Studios. The neon sign and building architecture in this area transport guests back to the 50's and 60's.

Detail 41: This is an early version travel trailer parked next to Restaurantosaurus in Dinoland USA in Animal Kingdom.

Detail 42: This is a sign to the Magic of Disney Animation Attraction in the Animation Courtyard in Disney's Hollywood Studios. Notice the tools of the trade that make up this sign: paint brush, pencil and film strip.

Detail 43: This is additional signage for Stitch's Great Escape in Tomorrowland in Magic Kingdom. The futuristic detailing of the signage and the metallic materials used in its construction transport guests into an alien environment!

Detail 44: This is a traffic light on Hollywood Boulevard in Disney's Hollywood Studios which adds to the feel of an earlier era and setting.

Detail 45: This is the Liberty Tree, an actual 100 year old tree, located in Liberty Square in Magic Kingdom. This tree was found on the original property of Walt Disney World and was transplanted to its current location during the park's construction. The lanterns that hang in the tree represent the original thirteen colonies. Additional information about the Liberty Tree can be found on a plaque near the tree.

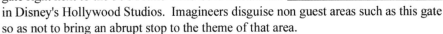

Detail 46: This is a battleship board ceiling in the shop across from the Toy Story Midway Mania Attraction in Pixar Place in Disney's Hollywood Studios. This whole area of the park is a wonderful flashback to the toys and games we all loved to play as kids!

Detail 47: This is the Echo Lake Apartments entry gate right next to the 50's Prime Time Cafe Restaurant in Disney's Hollywood Studios. Imagineers disguise non guest areas such as this gate so as not to bring an abrupt stop to the theme of that area.

Detail 48: This is a display of props just before you enter the France Pavilion in World Showcase in EPCOT. Look down to the right along the ledge as you cross over the last bridge into France from the United Kingdom. Take a close look at the painting on the easel and see if you recognize the scene which is across the way.

Detail 49: This lantern and stonework is at the Fairytale Garden Theatre which is hidden to the right of the castle between Fantasyland and Tomorrowland in Magic Kingdom. It is across from Cosmic Ray's Starlight Cafe and features Storytime with Belle as she tells her story about a Beast!

Detail 50: This is Gertie the Dinosaur found at the edge of Echo Lake near the Indiana Jones Epic Stunt Spectacular Attraction entrance in Disney's Hollywood Studios. This dinosaur is an example of programmatic architecture: the use of the dinosaur form as a building for a soft serve ice cream stand. It has also been said that this dinosaur is a reference to the 1914 American animated short, Gertie the Dinosaur, by Winsor McCay. This film set a standard that would be later carried on by Walt Disney and other animators by giving character to an animated animal.

Detail 51: This tree was the centerpiece for Pooh's Playful Spot in Fantasyland in Magic Kingdom from 2005 - 2010. The tree has been moved to the entrance of the Many Adventures of Winnie the Pooh Attraction due to a major Fantasyland expansion that has removed this playground.

Detail 52: This is the General Store near the Country Bear Jamboree Attraction in Frontierland in Magic Kingdom. It is covered in period details from the millwork on the porch, to the horse rail out front to tie off your ride as you come into town!

Detail 53: This is the facade of Brer Rabbit's house at the Briar Patch store located in the side of the Splash Mountain Attraction in Frontierland in Magic Kingdom.

Detail 54: This is Snow White's wishing well found on the left side of the Germany Pavilion in World Showcase in EPCOT. The best known version of this fairy tale came from Germany and so it seems the proper setting for this detail.

Detail 55: This clock is a centerpiece on the central tower facade of the Biergarten Restaurant in the Germany Pavilion in World Showcase in EPCOT.

Detail 56: These are the rats from the fountain near the entrance to the Muppet Vision 3-D Attraction in the Streets of America area in Disney's Hollywood Studios filling their boat with loot. Take a closer look at the rat in the front of the boat fishing for the coins thrown into the fountain by guests!

Detail 57: This is a tower fort along the edge of the Rivers of America near the Country Bear Jamboree Attraction in Frontierland in Magic Kingdom.

Detail 58: These are the horse shoes hanging on the structure of a past attraction loading area, known as the Mike Fink Keel Boats, at the edge of the Rivers of America in the Liberty Square area in Magic Kingdom. This boat ride attraction was based on Disney television shows and movies that featured Davy Crockett and it opened with the park in 1971. After problems arose with the boats, this attraction closed in 1997 and the loading area is now used primarily for stroller parking.

Detail 59: This detail is along the Maharajah Jungle Trek at the Bat Cliffs in Asia in Animal Kingdom. Imagineers have done their homework again with the props and details surrounding the guests so they become immersed into this setting.

Detail 60: This spear and shield prop is on the railing of the bridge leading into Adventureland in Magic Kingdom.

Detail 61: This planter is found in front of the Jungle Cruise Attraction area in Adventureland in Magic Kingdom. Imagineers make a planter out of what looks like a wooden cargo box with faded stencil lettering of an exotic plant company. This adds to the attraction itself and the theme of the surrounding land.

Detail 62: This lamp post is found at the crossover from the bridge entrance of Adventureland to Liberty Square in Magic Kingdom. Imagineers give a foreshadowing of the area ahead with the colonial style materials and construction used for this light pole.

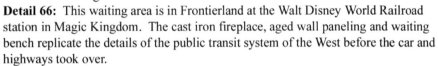

~ ANSWERS ~

Detail 63: This Kidcot Fun Stop station is at the American Pavilion in World Showcase in EPCOT and is decked out in details from the colonial period. These Kidcot stations are located throughout EPCOT and provide a nice break for children as they decorate a keepsake.

Detail 64: This snowman is located just down from the Toy Story Pizza Planet Arcade in the Streets of America area in Disney's Hollywood Studios.

Detail 65: This easy to spot telephone booth is located in the United Kingdom Pavilion in EPCOT.

Detail 66: This waiting area is in Frontierland at the Walt Disney World Railroad station in Magic Kingdom. The cast iron fireplace, aged wall paneling and waiting bench replicate the details of the public transit system of the West before the car and highways took over.

Detail 67: This is Push, the talking trash can and radio controlled robot that interacts with guests in the Tomorrowland area in Magic Kingdom. Usually surrounded by children trying to figure out how it works, Push is a regular steel lined trash can with a plastic bag insert that hides the robotic system and transmitter. Other interactive robots like Push include Wes Palm, a talking Palm Tree, and Pipa, another talking trash can, located in Animal Kingdom.

Detail 68: "Warning Do Not Pull Rope" - Yes the Imagineers DO want you to pull this rope at the well located to the left of the Indiana Jones Epic Stunt Spectacular Attraction in the Echo Lake area in Disney's Hollywood Studios. So next time you walk past this detail do pull and see what happens!

Detail 69: This is the Gossip phone located in the Chapeau Shop off of Main Street USA in Magic Kingdom. Search the store and once you find it, pick it up to hear the latest gossip!

Detail 70: This is the flock of seagulls at the entrance area of the Living Seas Pavilion on the west side of Future World in EPCOT. Imagineers bring life to this entrance area with the insisting chatter of "Mine, Mine, Mine!" that these birds are famous for in the 2003 animated hit Finding Nemo.

Detail 71: This is one of the fiberoptic paving panels on the walkway area between Innoventions and Spaceship Earth in EPCOT. It is an amazing detail of color and surprise as guests walk along this path in Future World at night.

Detail 72: These are the dinosaur foot prints at the Echo Lake area in Disney's Hollywood Studios. They cross the pavement into the grass and lead guests right to the culprit, Gertie the Dinosaur!

66

Detail 73: These are the horseshoe imprints in the pavement just inside the exit area of the Haunted Mansion Attraction in Liberty Square in Magic Kingdom. These prints must belong to the ghost horse harnessed to the black hearse nearby.

Detail 74: This is Minnie Mouse's signature and prints found with others just inside the courtyard of the Grauman's Chinese Theatre behind the Sorcerer's Hat on Hollywood Boulevard in Disney's Hollywood Studios. There are more prints to see in this Disney version walk of fame!

Detail 75: This heart is on the sidewalk in front of Tony's Town Square Restaurant in Town Square in Magic Kingdom. This Italian restaurant is themed after the 1955 animated film Lady and the Tramp. As you can see the theme flows out onto the sidewalk. Be sure to check out the details inside!

Detail 76: This is the gem filled pavement around the Magic Carpets of Aladdin Attraction in Adventureland in Magic Kingdom. Don't get too greedy because these gems are not real but a worthy aggregate to continue the theme for this area.

Detail 77: This odd pattern of paving is found throughout Liberty Square in Magic Kingdom and it definitely raises one's curiosity if noticed. So next time you are in the area see if you can find out why it is there!

Detail 78: This is a wall of sea monsters placed to the left of the Norway Pavilion in World Showcase in EPCOT. These creatures are often mentioned in that country's ancient lore of sea exploration.

Detail 79: This topiary serpent can be found down by the water just to the right of the hub towards Tomorrowland in Magic Kingdom. Take a close look at the shrubbery throughout the parks as they resemble different characters and creatures in this green thumb art form!

Detail 80: This bug is part of a bigger picture, one of conservation, at the entrance to Animal Kingdom's Conservation Station at Rafiki's Planet Watch. This is the facade that greets guests when they enter the building.

Detail 81: This is just one of the many architectural details found throughout the Walt Disney World Parks. This particular detail is the cornice work found along the parapet of the Morocco Pavilion in World Showcase in EPCOT.

Detail 82: This uniquely detailed post is found at the Hub in Magic Kingdom and shows that Walt and his Imagineers look into all details concerning their designs. This tradition continues today as the parks transform and expand.

Detail 83: This very playful section of buildings is in Dinoland USA in Animal Kingdom. Along with the vibrant colors are the building details which take on the characteristics of various animals.

Detail 84: This is the fountain statue of Cinderella and her friends found just to the left of the castle as you exit the tunnel into Fantasyland in Magic Kingdom. Notice how Cinderella is dressed in her peasant clothes and the crown on the background is alluding to her future as a princess. This is an exceptional detail that adds to the enjoyment of the guests' experience when they notice this correlation.

Detail 85: This is the mermaid fountain that was used in the 1984 hit movie Splash and can be found near the entrance to the Studio Backlot Tour Attraction in the Streets of America area in Disney's Hollywood Studios.

Detail 86: This beautiful mural is located inside the tunnel of Cinderella's Castle in Magic Kingdom. This and adjacent murals show the story of Cinderella as guests pass from the hub into Fantasyland.

Detail 87: This mural is found along the entry walls to the Land Pavilion on the west side of Future World in EPCOT.

Detail 88: This Robo Newz stand is found near the entrance to the TTA (Tomorrowland Transit Authority) in Tomorrowland in Magic Kingdom. Imagineers continue the galactic theme and storyline of this futuristic land with a look at what the news boy will evolve into.

Detail 89: This is the effects generator next to the Muppet Vision 3-D Attraction in the Streets of America in Disney's Hollywood Studios. Imagineers have a little fun with this Muppet themed area.

Detail 90: These pipes are located on the back side of the Muppet Vision 3-D Attraction in the Streets of America in Disney's Hollywood Studios. Imagineers have taken this opportunity to add even more detail to their story by adding some colorful painting and symbols to this typical building system located in an area that most guests walk right by without noticing.

Detail 91: This beanstalk is outside of the Sir Mickey's gift shop located in Fantasyland, just behind the castle, in Magic Kingdom. This shop is themed with details from the Mickey and the Beanstalk segment of the animated film Fun and Fancy Free, that was originally released to theatres in 1947. Be sure to look in this shop for a giant detail!

Detail 92: This is the Barber Shop found on the left side of Town Square, between the Emporium and Car Barn, as you enter into Magic Kingdom.

Detail 93: This is the backward waterfall which fits in perfectly with the Imagination Pavilion on the west side of Future World in EPCOT.

Detail 94: This river detail is found between Liberty Square and Frontierland in Magic Kingdom and runs from a silver plate out into the Rivers of America. This detail creates a transition between the two lands and their architecture. Furthermore, it represents the Mississippi River which separates the Colonial style of the East coast from the booming growth of the frontier to the West.

Detail 95: This is Walt's window located above the Plaza Ice Cream Palor on Main Street USA facing the castle in Magic Kingdom. The reason given for this location was that Walt loved ice cream and the window overlooked his beloved castle. Imagineers have used the windows on Main Street to comemorate many people who had a part in the making of this park. Next time you walk down Main Street, take a look at the unique way that people are remembered!

Detail 96: This is the Academy of Television Arts & Sciences Hall of Fame located to the left of the American Idol Experience Attraction in the Echo Lake area in Disney's Hollywood Studios. It contains busts of famous entertainers including Walt Disney himself.

Detail 97: This is the statue of Roy O. Disney sitting on a park bench with Minnie Mouse which is found in the central courtyard of Town Square in Magic Kingdom. After Walt Disney's untimely death, his brother Roy watched over the construction of Disney World in Orlando, Florida. At its completion, Roy renamed the park, "Walt Disney World," as a tribute to his brother.

Detail 98: This is Cinderella's Castle in Magic Kingdom. It is adorned with glimmering icicle lights which can be seen during the Christmas holidays and is a breathtaking sight in the night sky! Imagineers transform the castle for different holidays and celebrations, but this ice overlay has to be among the most dazzling!

Detail 99: This is a wall of tombs found in the exit area of the Haunted Mansion Attraction in Liberty Square in Magic Kingdom. Imagineers add some comic relief to this morbid setting with a play on words.

There are many of these details throughout the attractions at the Walt Disney World Parks and each add additional enjoyment to the guest's experience. If you have enjoyed this Attention to Detail compilation, please keep your eyes peeled for our book which focuses on attractions.

Disney Detail Park Breakdown

For your convenience, we have gathered the Disney Details in this book with the park that you can find them in.

Magic Kingdom Park:
05, 08, 10, 11, 14, 17, 18, 19, 25, 27, 29, 30, 33, 37, 43, 45, 49, 51, 52, 53, 57, 58, 60, 61, 62, 66, 67, 69, 73, 75, 76, 77, 79, 82, 84, 86, 88, 91, 92, 94, 95, 97, 98, 99

Animal Kingdom Park:
06, 12, 13, 15, 16, 34, 38, 41, 59, 80, 83

EPCOT:
02, 03, 09, 21, 22, 24, 26, 31, 32, 48, 54, 55, 63, 65, 70, 71, 78, 81, 87, 93

Disney's Hollywood Studios:
01, 04, 07, 20, 23, 28, 35, 36, 39, 40, 42, 44, 46, 47, 50, 56, 64, 68, 72, 74, 85, 89, 90, 96

Walt Disney was always looking at his parks and thinking about ways to improve them. With that in mind it must be noted that as the parks evolve, change and update some of the details shown in this book may change or even disappear.

Commission:

Now that you have seen these 99 images, there is always room for one more!
We hope this book has opened your eyes
to view what Walt Disney and his Imagineers
have created for each of us to encounter and enjoy
at the Walt Disney World Parks in Orlando, Florida.
So in future visits we hope you will pay
Attention To Detail.

Attention to Detail
Magic Kingdom Hunt

Object:
To seek, find, and capture a picture of as many of the twelve details contained in this Magic Kingdom Hunt within the time limit set.

Time Limit:
90 minutes

Rules:
1) Group into teams with each team having a camera device.
2) Select a location to meet at when the time expires.
3) One member must take a picture of the other team members with the detail. The same person does not have to always take the pictures but all other team members must be in the picture.
4) Gather together to see which team was able to seek, find and capture the most Disney Details with their team.

Reminder:
Don't forget to make a copy of this hunt for each team if they do not have their own book. Also, be careful not to interfere or disturb other guests at the park while you engage in the scavenger hunt.

Variations:
- You can vary the time limit to fit your schedule or just hunt throughout the day.
- You can hunt by yourself or with teams.
- You can prepare ahead in finding the images or not look at them until the hunt starts.
- Turn on the date/time stamp on your cameras to see who took the pictures the fastest or within the time limit.

Turn the page to get started

12 Magic Kingdom Details await

Seek, Find and Click!

MK001.1 - Tomorrowland
MK001.2 - Fantasyland
MK001.3 - Adventureland
MK001.4 - Frontierland
MK001.5 - Main Street
MK001.6 - Fantasyland
MK001.7 - Adventureland
MK001.8 - Hub
MK001.9 - Frontierland
MK001.10 - Main Street
MK001.11 - Tomorrowland
MK001.12 - Town Square

Object:
Using the thirty-three phrases below take a picture of what Disney detail comes to your mind while in the parks. You can do this in groups or by yourself; in a set amount of time or during the length of your trip. The main rule is to just have fun and be creative!

1 - show a little character
2 - tea for two
3 - lots of spots
4 - street of dreams
5 - hats off to you
6 - that's just goofy!
7 - be our guest
8 - give a little whistle
9 - beautiful tomorrow
10 - it will come around
11 - draw me close
12 - what time is it?
13 - ready, set, go!
14 - tools of the trade
15 - mirror, mirror, on the wall
16 - not my size
17 - rain, rain, go away
18 - how do you do?
19 - make a wish!
20 - perfect fit
21 - I'm stuffed
22 - are you "fur" real?
23 - true blue
24 - under the sea
25 - what's your point?
26 - let's roll
27 - one bad apple
28 - green with envy
29 - that will leave a mark
30 - what's that smell?
31 - it's over my head
32 - pretty in pink
33 - dreams come true

About the Authors

Keith Black ~ Author/Graphics

Keith Black became introduced to the world of Disney after visiting Walt Disney World with his wife and two young daughters back in 2003. He quickly realized the wonderful family environment the resort offered and has taken his family back each year. With his background in architecture and engineering Keith has been intrigued with the life's work of Walt Disney and his Imagineers.

Favorite Park:	Magic Kingdom
Favorite Time to visit:	Fall
Favorite Details:	
Level 1:	Detail 10
Level 2:	Detail 42
Level 3:	Detail 84

Jacquelyn Damon ~ CoAuthor/Photographer

Jackie Damon is a veteran visitor to Walt Disney World. During her first visit in 1973 her love for the Disney Parks began and continued to grow to include everything at this special place. Jackie has always had a great interest in photography and enjoys capturing the many unique details all around Walt Disney World to share with others.

Favorite Park:	Magic Kingdom
Favorite Time to visit:	Winter
Favorite Details:	
Level 1:	Detail 33
Level 2:	Detail 51
Level 3:	Detail 95